SQUEEZING BIRTH INTO WORKING LIFE

Squeezing Birth into Working Life

Household panel data analyses comparing Germany,
Great Britain, Sweden and The Netherlands

CÉCILE WETZELS
University of Amsterdam
and TNO-Institute of Strategy, Technology and Policy,
Delft, The Netherlands

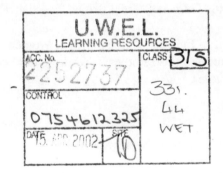
Ashgate

Aldershot • Burlington USA • Singapore • Sydney

Published by
Ashgate Publishing Ltd
Gower House
Croft Road
Aldershot
Hants GU11 3HR
England

Ashgate Publishing Company
131 Main Street
Burlington, VT 05401-5600 USA

Ashgate website: http://www.ashgate.com

British Library Cataloguing in Publication Data
Wetzels, Cécile
   Squeezing birth into working life : household panel data
   analyses comparing Germany, Great Britain, Sweden and the
   Netherlands
   1. Work and family - Europe - Case studies 2. Women -
   Employment - Europe - Case studies 3. Working mothers -
   Europe - Case studies
   I. Title
   306.8'743

Library of Congress Control Number: 00-131256

ISBN 0 7546 1232 5

Printed and bound by Athenaeum Press, Ltd.,
Gateshead, Tyne & Wear.

Contents

List of Tables and Figures

Preface

This book is a slightly revised version of my doctoral thesis defended at the University of Amsterdam on January 21, 1999. Siv Gustafsson attracted me to the research on fertility, female labour supply and public policies. Having studied a completely different field, strategies of organisation at the economics department of Tilburg University, the spirit of the researchers working on Population and Gender Economics at the University of Amsterdam gave an interesting and stimulating encouragement to survey the field.

Participation in the European women's labour force network in 1995 at once revealed the structure of what the thesis should capture. At that time I made the following choices. First I chose to analyse women's labour force behaviour in a short term perspective and detailed, by making use of panel data on women's own human capital and monthly labour market behaviour and their spouse's human capital and labour market behaviour. Secondly I chose to analyse women's birth labour market behaviour and timing of giving birth, by birth order. Thirdly I chose a country comparative perspective to reveal effects of different public policy packages in addition to effects explained by human capital theory.

The research required comparable household panel data sets between countries. The course on 'Using equivalent household data files' at the Center for Policy Research, Maxwell School of Citizenship and Public Affairs, at Syracuse University New York sponsored by National Institute on Ageing and Deutsches Institut fur Wirtschaftsforschung (DIW) was important to understand the data management. The data collection was performed in Germany at DIW Berlin, in Great Britain at ESRC Essex University, in Sweden at Gothenborg University and for The Netherlands at Stichting Organisatie voor Strategisch Arbeidsmarktonderzoek, in the Hague/Tilburg.

In the European Labour Force network I very much appreciated to work with Jan Dirk Vlasblom (from DIW, Berlin) and Andrew McCullough and Shirley Dex (ESRC, Essex University/Cambridge University). In 1997 I became affiliated with the Stichting Organisatie voor Strategisch Arbeidsmarktonderzoek till January 1999. Marian de Voogd-Hamelink's interest, and knowledge of the panel data set, has proved to be beneficial for my research purposes. Thanks to her!

Siv Gustafsson has been for four PhD years an intelligent and wise supervisor. It is a great fortune that we have become friends and an inspired and productive team. Immediately after the thesis defence the Economics Department at the University of Amsterdam employed me to extend the research. The first extension concerns the analyses of postponement of first birth in connection with labour force behaviour by comparing time periods. This project includes Eiko Kenjoh who started to work on her PhD thesis in September 1998. A second extension is the research on supply side dynamics regarding non-standard work arrangements around childbearing using the household panel data for Germany, Great Britain, The Netherlands and Sweden. A third extension is the analysis of dead weight loss of the Dutch childcare system, which is between government, firms and parents, compared to the public day-care system in Sweden. Simone Dobbelsteen is a good companion in this project.

The research laid out in this thesis and the further development of the analyses would have been much harder without the moral support and ever lasting love of my parents, sisters, and best friends. Special thanks go to the following friends: René Almekinders for patience and software package knowledge, Jacqueline Martina for improving my English, Susan van Velzen for valuable critical remarks on chapter 2, Mary Morgan for sharing interest in notions in econom(etr)ic theory, and finally Marcel van der Linde for explaining individual law cases, which clarified both limits and power of my own work. I also enjoyed his reading of Keri Hulme's and Ben Okri's works to me after hard work and painful eyes.

Currently I am affiliated with the Dutch Organisation for Applied Scientific Research in Delft. I hope this book shares your interest and knowledge, and contributes to both.

Cécile Wetzels, Amsterdam 2000.

1 Introduction

*Children are usually not purchased but are self-produced by each
family, using market goods and services and the own time of parents,
especially of mothers*

Becker, 1981: 96

Subject and relevance

At a time when women in industrialised countries have a stronger and more
permanent presence in the labour market than ever before, how do births fit
into a young woman's curriculum vitae? In this book several aspects of
women's labour market behaviour in connection with childbearing are
analysed. First, we analyse labour force transitions in connection with child
birth. Secondly, we analyse women's share in joint family earnings around
the birth of the first and second child. Thirdly, we analyse the timing of
having the first child and subsequent children in connection with labour
force attachment of women. Fourth we focus on the optimal age of
maternity considering career costs by studying the (potential) age earnings
curves of women.

Today, most economists and other social scientists as well as
politicians will readily admit both the importance of female paid careers in
society and the importance of healthy young mothers and new born
children. Employers also have an interest in happy and healthy employees.
Both individual women and governments may be interested in securing that
women may be mothers without having to sacrifice their financial
independence. Particularly this has become an issue in connection with
single mothers to what extent they have to rely on tax revenue financed
social benefits rather than on their own earned income. and at what age of
the child is it acceptable that the mother has no earned income from labour
market work? The same type of reasoning applies to married women
although in this case it is more common to accept the view that division of
work within the family can allow the married woman to be a full-time
home maker for most of her life. Increasingly, women do not accept this
role for themselves but want to increase their own economic independence
as well as develop their own human resources into a labour market career.

From the child's point of view it is desirable that parents have enough time to care for and develop the child's psychic and physical wellbeing. This consideration is a reason for aspiring mothers and fathers not to renter the labour force too early after having a child and not for too many hours of work per week. From the government's point of view expenditures on child care by own parents or others, which enhance the cognitive development of young children, may be justified, since long term productivity in an economy may be affected (Blau and Grossberg, 1990).

Public policies have been designed to influence the re-entering decision of the mother and the father. These policies include maternity benefits, paid parental leaves, job security during a pre and post birth period and subsidised day care which allow parents to combine work and family responsibilities. Thus policies are on the one hand designed to allow parents time with their young children and on the other hand to allow mothers not to lose contact with the labour market for ever. Until now very few fathers make use of opportunities to reduce work hours to care for their own children. This is the main reason why this book concentrates on women and gives only a secondary role to men.

The contribution to social science research on women's labour market behaviour, this book aims at, is three fold. First, the subjects are analysed in a welfare state comparative perspective. The focus of study includes four countries namely Germany, Sweden, The Netherlands and the United Kingdom. Secondly, a birth and work histories file has been created on a monthly basis by making use of all available waves of the household panel data from the four countries. The fertility and work files are organised around the same moment in women's family building cycle, namely at the point of having a child. Thirdly, we analyse policy relevant issues in a comparative perspective making use of these fertility and work history files.

Positioning in the scientific field

Our hypotheses on women's labour market behaviour in the period they (time to) have a child are derived from human capital theory, theory on labour supply and micro economic theory of fertility. In addition, we believe that different public policy on the family will make women with the same human capital behave differently between countries. This approach contrasts with the usual functional approach in most economic thinking, which emphasises social policy design as the result of solving a problem: if all four countries have industrial market economies, one would expect similarity in the problems and therefore in the solutions. However there may not be a strong uniqueness to the solution of common problems.

The position of the analyses on the timing of maternity and spacing of children is in the field of population economics with a relevance for gender issues. Population economics can be defined as using the economic approach to demographic issues such as the behaviour of birth rates. Related public policy issues such as family policies: child care, taxation systems, social benefits are of relevance to the outcomes. The theoretical approach is micro economics of the family (e.g. Cigno 1991). Decisions about the timing of births are influenced by economic factors such as opportunity costs of time, which primarily consist of labour market income forgone and investments in human capital forgone.

What differences do welfare state variations make for women with the similar human capital, who are in the same stage of their family building life cycle? In exploring this question it is important to examine countries that represent a broad array of variations. Accordingly, the analysis here deals with Germany, The Netherlands, Sweden and the United Kingdom. The welfare states of these countries differ in significant ways. Furthermore, these countries started to collect household panel data sets, with similar, individual household member's information on labour market behaviour and fertility behaviour, on a monthly level, from the 1980s onwards. These data sets allow the empirical analyses of Chapters 4-7. Similar information has not yet been available for other European countries, although recently household panels are becoming available also for Poland, Hungary and Italy.

Data

The empirical analyses in this book are based on the fertility and work history files, which have been constructed for this purpose from the German Socio Economic Panel (GSOEP), the British Household Panel Study (BHPS), the Swedish HUShällens ekonomiska levnadsförhällanden (HUS) and the Dutch labour supply panel collected by the Organisatie voor Strategisch Arbeidsmarktonderzoek (OSA). We organised the data on women's labour market status with the date of birth of children as a starting point. Human capital variables are based on the date of childbearing or some period before and after the date of childbearing. Human capital variables have been made compatible between countries. Since Germany,

Great Britain, Sweden and The Netherlands started to collect household panel data from the mid 1980s onwards, we make use of data on the household situation and labour market situation of household members over a period of ten years. Women's position is our starting point, the person the woman is living with, will be included in the analyses as her spouse.

Outline

The following is a brief guide through the contents of the book: Chapter 2 gives the most important differences between Germany, Sweden, The Netherlands and the United Kingdom regarding policies that affect women's combination of work and children. Chapter 3 describes how we constructed fertility and work history files from national household data sets of Germany, Great Britain, Sweden and The Netherlands.

Chapter 4 is a revised version of an article published in a special issue of the Journal of Population Economics (1996). In Chapter 4 the following questions are answered in a welfare state comparative perspective: What is the labour force status at several points in time around the birth of children according to child order? What determines whether a woman is a continuous career person i.e. if she participates on the labour market both 3 months before giving birth and 24 months after giving birth? What are the determinants of the time till the woman is back on the labour market after childbearing? We find that women's capital endowment and the income of the spouse explain an important part of women's career orientation.

Chapter 5 is a contribution to the research on the effect of children on women's career and earnings. Different from most research along these lines we study a more short term effect of a childbirth on earnings rather than the long run effect, which has been studied previously. We believe that the most vulnerable period in a woman's career and her future capability of providing for herself is the time immediately around childbearing. The degree to which earning and mothering can be made compatible is crucial for these effects. We analyse earnings of women as the share in total earned household income before and after the birth of children. We analyse the determinants of share of earnings of the wife decomposed into predicted wage, probability of labour force participation and predicted hours of work, simplifying the analysis by assuming husband's income to be exogenous. We hypothesise that human capital, accumulated before having children, will determine earnings during and after mothering of pre-school children. Most studies in female labour supply include variables on family composition, number of children and children's age. Our study differs from these studies in that we selected the women at precisely the same moment in their family building cycle namely at the point of having their first child. In addition we carry out a simulation to compare labour supply behaviour between Sweden and Germany.

Chapters 6 and 7 deal with the relation between accumulated human capital and the timing of births in a woman's life, and explain women's age at maternity and the age at having a subsequent child, whereas in chapters 4 and 5 age at giving birth had been regarded as exogenous. Chapter 6 presents the decisions on the timing and spacing of children in a woman's life in West Germany, Great Britain and Sweden.

Chapter 7 estimates the gains in life time earnings by education that Dutch women have made by postponement of maternity. We analyse Dutch women's potential age earnings curves, women's wages before and after giving birth and, labour force participation and hours of work after giving birth. An earlier version of Chapter 6 has been published in Gustafsson and Wetzels (1997). The analyses of Chapter 6 and 7 have been developed in a four country comparison in Gustafsson and Wetzels (2000), Gustafsson, Wetzels and Kenjoh (forthcoming). Chapter 8 concludes with a summary of the main findings.

2   Breadwinner Ideology against Individual and Equal Role Sharing Ideology

Some Socialists think, ere the century's fled,
That wealth will be much less unequally spread:
Well, we hope so ! but still, as we all understand,
A bird in the bush is not one in the hand.
Reckless increase, to wilfully aggravate needs,
Some advise just to starve men to desperate deeds;
The Socialist programme, by making afraid,
To impose on their fellows they cannot persuade

Till my income increase and I'm quite at my ease,
My children shall not, if the Socialist please!
That I may afford twelve under Socialist rule,
Is no reason for having them now as a fool.
Such increase in numbers is morally wrong,
It takes comforts from children to whom they belong.

J.R. (1887,3) in The Malthusian[1]

---

[1]   Journal of the British birth control movement. The poem reflects the discussions between Socialists and (neo)Malthus(ians). An analysis of these discussions and the contribution of feminists, is given in Wetzels (1994). The central idea put forward by Malthus in 'The Essay on the Principle of Population, as it affects the future improvement of society with remarks on the speculations of Mr Godwin, Mr Condorcet, and other writers' (1798), is that fertility is an increasing function of income. This was not explicitly based on the assumption that the demand for children is positively related to income, but rather Malthus assumed that the individual's preference for marriage and a mate are given, and he reasoned that social constraints allowed this preference to be satisfied only when individuals could properly support a family, namely when they had sufficient income. From these microrelationships it followed that there should be a macro relationship between per capita income and population growth, and to this Malthus appended the accepted concept of diminishing returns to labour, where land is relatively fixed in supply.

Introduction

The main empirical concern of this study is to examine women's labour market behaviour in the period they (time to) have a child. Human capital accumulated by the woman helps to explain this behaviour in this particular period in a woman's life. Before children are born women's labour force participation rates are high. Whether a woman will leave the labour market in the period when her children are born, will from an economics perspective depend on the loss of earnings if she leaves the labour market to care for the child, the loss of earnings if the father/her spouse leaves the labour market to care for the child, the costs of care for the child by some other person (child care costs) and the pleasure of parents to care for their own child relative to the pleasure they derive from market work.

Different public policy on the family will make women with the same human capital behave differently between countries. What differences do welfare state variations make for women with similar human capital, who are in the same stage of their family building life cycle? In exploring this question it is important to examine countries that represent a broad array of variations. Accordingly, the analysis here deals with Germany, Sweden, The Netherlands and the United Kingdom. The welfare states of these countries differ in significant ways and there are comparable household and individual data in detail from the 1980s onwards that allow the empirical analyses of Chapters 4-7.

In clarifying differences in governmental policies on the family in Germany,[2] The Netherlands, Sweden and the United Kingdom, we first apply Esping-andersen's (mainstream) welfare state typology (1990). This typology concerns different ideologies behind the role of the state, and whether welfare benefits are based on the principles of need, market work performance or citizenship. In addition to this mainstream perspective, we need Sainsbury's (1994,1996) gender perspective on welfare state variations, to analyse the impact of the welfare state on women and men or the differences in impact, and the disparities in welfare provision between

---

[2]   The German public policies on the family described in this chapter apply to former West Germany. Former East German policy on the family is included in Chapter 4, which presents the only analysis of the East German data in this study. Since German unification in 1989, policies of West Germany apply to the whole of Germany.

the sexes. Sainsbury makes the distinction between the breadwinner typology as against the individual and equal role sharing typology in social policy, by applying the principles of maintenance or care.

Public policies on the family such as the taxation regime and social premium payments affect after tax earnings per hour (per individual household member). Employees' right to work part time and public expenditures on 'special' benefits for parents and their children in the period of childbearing such as paid parental leave, job protection period, available subsidised good quality child care, may aim at labour force attachment of both spouses or stimulate specialisation within the household in a (paid) child carer, and a 'market worker'.

Furthermore, the effects of different measures of public policies on the family on the labour market performance of those making use of it may be twofold. Parental leave programs whether they are paid or not, may decrease labour market contact, whereas institutional child care may increase labour market contact. The net effect is uncertain, and we will not be able in this study to further investigate the effects of different measures within public policy of the family.

Since the main empirical concern of this study only gives a secondary role to men, the gender perspective helps to concentrate on women's labour market position (and hourly earnings) in the period they (time to) have children. In this way we do not have a clear focus on equal role sharing within households. Future work may fill this gap.

This chapter is organised as follows. We start by characterising public policies on the family in the countries included, first by applying Esping-andersen mainstream typology (1990). Secondly, the degree of breadwinner orientation of public involvement in work and family, as inspired by Sainsbury (1994). Then, we present actual public policies on the family in Germany, Sweden, The Netherlands and the United Kingdom during the period we analyse empirically in Chapters 4-7. Actual policies in the four countries describe the situation by mid 1990s. We discuss expectations derived from differing public policies on the family on the labour force attachment of women during the period they plan and actually have children. Finally, we present conclusions.

Social Policy Ideologies 1: principle of need, market work performance and citizenship

A central assumption in Esping-andersen's typology is that welfare states can be understood only through their historical ideology, and that the ideological legacy shapes the present day actions of policy makers. Based on this reasoning three different types of clusters of capitalist welfare states are distinguished: the liberal or residualist, the conservative or corporatist, and the social democratic or institutional. Whereas Esping-andersen worked out his typology mainly for pensions, sickness benefits and the creation of jobs in the public sector, this chapter applies his typology to public involvement (funding) in policies on the combination of children and paid work. The three types of welfare states are not to be seen as pure cases but as approximations, where a particular country has more defining characteristics of one of the three types welfare states than of the other two types.

The first type of welfare state, the liberal welfare state, is characterised by a belief that the unfettered market brings welfare to the maximum number of citizens. Only if the market fails to do so the state will intervene with welfare benefits which are typically means tested and often carry a social stigma.

The second type of welfare state is shaped by a corporatist statist legacy with a strong influence of the church. '(...) the corporatist regimes are (...) typically shaped by the church and hence strongly committed to the preservation of traditional familyhood. Social insurance typically excludes non-working wives, and family benefits encourage motherhood [unpaid child care by the mother]. Day care and similar family services, are conspicuously underdeveloped; the principle of 'subsidiarity' serves to emphasise that the state will only interfere when family's capacity to service its members is exhausted' (Esping-Andersen, 1990:27). Welfare state provisions are typically organised along occupational lines, often with preferential treatment of civil servants.

In the third type of welfare state, the social democratic welfare state, welfare provisions are institutional, seldom means tested and usually apply to all citizens alike. 'Perhaps the most salient characteristic of the social democratic regime is its fusion between welfare and work. It is at once genuinely committed to a full employment guarantee, and entirely dependent on its attainment.' (Esping-Andersen, 1990:28).

In Table 2.1 we characterise the governmental policies on the family in Germany, The Netherlands, Sweden and the United Kingdom according to Esping-andersen's typology. Specifically we pay attention to the maternity leave period and maternity benefits, and to public involvement in provision of childcare. Leave regulations due to childbearing are separated into pregnancy leave and maternity leave in Germany and The Netherlands, whereas in the United Kingdom the leave starts when being pregnant and ends while caring (a combination of pregnancy leave and maternity leave), and in Sweden the leave starts when the child is born, which means that there is only maternity leave.[3]

A second difference between the countries is the eligibility of individual parents to leave and benefits. Whereas British fathers are not eligible, Dutch mothers and fathers have individual rights to parental leave, and German and Swedish parents have a right to share the leave as they choose themselves. If parents are both eligible maternity leave is called parental leave, but since Britain has a leave regulation for mothers only and in the other countries the leave is mainly taken by women, we will in the following label the leave period after the child is born 'maternity leave'.

United Kingdom

Public involvement in combining work and family is minimal in the United Kingdom compared to the family policies in West Germany, Sweden and in The Netherlands from 1990. Britain's leave period for pregnancy and maternity is 40 weeks, of which during 6 weeks about 90% of earnings is replaced, during 12 weeks about 20% of earnings is replaced.

---

[3]   There is a special pregnancy leave and benefit regulation in Sweden of 60 days with 90% of earnings (50 days before child delivery and 10 days after the child is born) that applies to women in physically demanding work.

Table 2.1:   Type of Welfare State and Family Policy Regime

Welfare State Typology	Liberal	Conservative, Christian Democrat		W-Germany	Social Democrat
Welfare state characteristic:	only if market fails the state will intervene.	only if family's capacity to service its members is exhausted, the state will intervene.			welfare provisions are institutional, and usually apply to all citizens alike
Country	**United Kingdom**	**The Netherlands** till 1990s	from 1990s	**W-Germany**	**Sweden**
Public family policies:	weak	weak	medium	strong	strong
Policy focus on	- need	- need	- childcare	- allowances in taxation	- childcare
	- children's education	- children's educ.	- women's lfp	- child benefits	- women's lfp
			- equal sharing paid and unpaid work between men and women		- equality between men and women
Maternity Leave					
women's total job protection[0]	medium	short	medium	long	long
income compensation during total job protection	low	high	only in public sector high	low	high
parental leave paid by[1]	employer	employer	employer 47[2] (1995)	tax money	tax money 90 (1988)
%taking paid parental leave					
Interruptions allowed			no, one period		yes, "banking system"[3]
Child Care					
subsidised full day child care	no	no	yes	no	yes
Full needs supply	no	no	no	no	yes
% of costs paid by parents[4]	0	n.a.	28	n.a.	13.4
% of children of ages 0-3[5]	2	n.a.	7.5	3	27
child's school age	5	4	4	6	7

Lfp = labour force participation; [0] total job protection means protection during pregnancy and parental leave; [1] pregnancy benefits are paid out of tax money in United Kingdom, Germany and The Netherlands; [2] 58% is taken by mothers and 35% by fathers; [3] Sundström (1996); [4] estimates by CBS (1991), Gustafsson and Stafford (1992); [5]SCP 1997: 124, figure for The Netherlands: Mutsaers (1997)

Thereafter there is no earnings compensation.[4] Fathers are not eligible, and there is no right to leave from work to care for sick children. British parents can only enjoy better provisions than the national standards if they work with an employer who has as a result of negotiations conceded to better provisions. Some of the more generous employers offer up to a year's paid maternity leave (Joshi, Macran and Dex, 1996).

Successive government ministers have specifically rejected the concept of any public responsibility in ensuring the availability of day care for working parents.[5] Child care services provided by employers were liable to taxation up to 1990 (OECD 1990:139). Apart from pre-primary education which is typically part day (2.5 hours per day), public provision of day care is therefore extremely limited. The state has mainly been involved in supervision e.g. the administration and inspection of care by child minders. British mothers on state benefits make free use of a space and have priority to publicly provided day care, along with lone parents.

In conclusion, we can say that in the family policy area United Kingdom is a typical example of the liberal welfare state.

---

[4]   McRae (1991) analyses for the period 1980-1989 the proportion of (working) mothers in Britain who are entitled to a very small maternity grant, and those working mothers who receive more benefits. In 1980 all British mothers received a maternity grant, 50% of all mothers received the maternity allowance and 30% of all mothers received the Earnings Related supplements (ERS). Among employed mothers 90% received the maternity allowance, and 50% received the ERS (18 weeks). In 1989, 40% of all mothers received some type of maternity pay, 20% of all mothers received 90% of earnings during 6 weeks. Among employed mothers 80% received some benefit, 65% received Statutory Maternity Pay (lower rate means on average 20% earnings of a full-time worker (EOC, 1991: 25), 40% received a higher rate. All flat rate benefits like the maternity grant, and allowance, are very low and not indexed for consumer prices.

[5]   See for example:
    "Daycare will continue to be primarily a matter of private arrangements between parents and private and voluntary resources except when there are special needs..." (John Patten, Hansard, March 18, 1985).
    "Our view is that it is for parents that go out to work to decide how best to care for their children. If they want to or need help in this they should make appropriate arrangements and meet the costs." (Edwina Currie, Hansard, July 12, 1988)
    "If you have to work you do and if you have to find child care you find it. When I say 'have' I mean if you really want to." (Angela Rumbold, Family Policy Bulletin, March, 1991).

The Netherlands

The Dutch family policy area is characterised as a corporatist Christian democratic welfare state, until 1994.[6] The influence of the pillarization,[7] the Catholic principle of subsidiarity and the Protestant doctrine's sphere of sovereignty, gave a central importance to traditional familyhood, determined by 24 hours presence by the mother in the home with the children (Moree, 1992), and a male breadwinner, earning a breadwinner's wage. Therborn (1989:206-8) characterises the Dutch state as weak and 'subsidiary' to the pillars. The hierarchical view of authority inherent in subsidiarity has placed the state above divisional interests; it has been envisioned as a higher agent in harmonising the conflicting interests of groups with the aim of maintaining their autonomy (Wilensky 1982:353). The state's responsibility to safeguard a social minimum is reflected in constitutional guarantee and the notion of the caring state (Hupe, 1993).

In 1930 employed women were granted 12 weeks of leave with 100% of payment. In international comparison this was rather early.[8] However, Dutch women did not have job protection for pregnancy, childbirth or marriage, till 1973. Parents fulfilled their specialised tasks within the traditional family model. Feminists, and employers who were in need of female employees demanded more (public) child care facilities.[9]

It lasted till the 1990s for Dutch public policy activity on the combination of work and family to become vivid, heading in more individual and institutional direction. In 1990 maternity leave was extended from 12 to 16 weeks and employees became eligible to parental leave of 6

---

[6]   In 1994, a new government was installed without representation of the Christian Democratic Party (CDA). The CDA had influenced the political agenda on family and work for a long time by advocating traditional family values, embracing mothers (unpaid) duties in the home. In 1997, the CDA party marketed itself again by defining the family in their political program (all other political programs did not give a definition on the family). The definition sounded: 'a household situation in which an adult takes long term responsibility over an other adult and/or to care and raise children' (CDA, 1997, 26-27).

[7]   By this expression is meant that society is organized into separate segments based on religious or political beliefs, where Roman Catholics and Calvinists made up the most important pillars and later socialists formed a separate pillar of their own.

[8]   In Sweden 12 weeks of maternity leave were granted in 1939, in Germany 14 weeks of maternity leave were granted in 1957.

[9]   Between 1965 and 1980 the number of child care centers, open a few hours per day, mostly a few days per week, increased from 100 to 3000. Tijdens and Lioen (1993) give a comprehensive overview of the history of organization of Dutch child care provision.

months part time from 1991 onwards.[10] The law on parental leave does not deal with the payment during leave, and leaves this to negotiations between employers and employees. In a few collective labour market agreements payment is taken care off, but the payment itself differs between the different agreements in Dutch called CAO from Centrale Arbeids Overeenkomst, of which there are about 900 in The Netherlands covering different sectors of the labour market. Most CAO's however do not cover paid parental leaves as many as 90% of all employees are covered by a CAO without payment of parental leave. However, the (CAO of the) public sector offers 75% of earnings, and 47% of all eligible parents take leave in this sector. In contrast, only 8% of eligible parents make use of their right to unpaid leave (Niphuis-Nell, 1997). Among all eligible parents 19% took leave during 1994-1996. Some negotiations also result in possibilities to take different number of leave hours per week combined with a different period of leave, for example 6 months 50% of weekly hours, 1 year 25% of weekly hours etc. However the leave period can only be taken without interruption. From July 1997 leave can be taken till the child is 8 years old and is also available for employees who work less than 20 hours per week. The Queen's speech (1998) indicated that a new law on leave including parental leave is in preparation (Kaderwet Arbeid en Zorg). Furthermore saving leave in time or money and the legal right to take leave for care remain on the political agenda.

The Childcare Stimulation Act of 1990 is the first government action which explicitly caters to the needs of the working mother rather than assigning priority to educational considerations for children. At first public involvement concentrated on child care for pre schoolers, which increased the percentage of children of ages 0-4 in child care from 3.3 in 1990 to 7.5 in 1995. Only 0.8% of children of ages 4-12 are in child care in 1995. However there are still waiting lists which Mutsaers (1997) estimates to be 32,000 full time child care places for children of all age groups. According to the Confederation of Dutch Communities (SGBO, 1997) the waiting lists

---

[10] Meanwhile German parental leave was extended to 6 months paid, in 1979 with a maximum of DM 750 per month, whereas Swedish parental leave was already 6 months in 1968 with 65% of earnings. The length of parental leave period and the benefit period was extended several times till 36 months leave with 24 months benefit in Germany in 1993 and 18 months with 18 months benefit in Sweden in the 1990s.

for children of ages 0-4 were estimated to be 23,000 full time places, and 10,000 for children of ages 4-13. Groot and Maassen van den Brink (1996) show that 84% of Dutch mothers use informal child care, of which 58% is unpaid.

Public involvement in childcare concerns the quality of child care and fiscal incentives for employers to create child care facilities, fiscal facilities for parents who use child care facilities. Fiscal measures will amount to Dfl 150 million in 2002. The Dutch government intends to stimulate employers to supply child care for their personnel by having municipalities give companies subsidies out of state subsidies.[11]

Childcare subsidies will be increased by Dfl 50 million in 1999, till Dfl 250 million in 2002, to increase child care capacity, including after school care capacity. Additional Dfl 60 million will be used to implement proposals of the commission on 'organisation of the combination of work and family'.[12] The government supports the scenario of an average working week of 29-32 hours for both women and men, with variation dependent on the life cycle. Also unpaid care work should be equally shared by men and women in future (SCP 1997:290).

Germany

Similar to The Netherlands, Germany is characterised as a Christian Democratic Welfare State, with a strong traditional familial ideology. The German tax system is expected implicitly to support traditional family formation, by giving a "marriage benefit" to all couples except to those couples where the husband and wife earn the same incomes.

In the period 1950-1960s conservative governments strengthened the family as an institution, installing the so called 'Duales System des Familienlastenausgleichs', with tax deductions for children and child benefits to ease the cost of children. From 1969-1982 social liberal governments abolished the tax deductions for children and aimed at more active involvement of women in the labour market introducing the maternity leave act in 1979. It was also during this period, namely in 1976, that a German woman became legally an equal partner in family decisions on financial issues. However, after this period conservative liberal

---

[11]   Dutch municipalities receive 95% of their income from the national state. In 1995 39% of child care spaces were rented by employers.

[12]   This commission was installed in November 1996 to develop proposals to improve working schedules and child care schedules, school holidays, opening hours of shops and services. The proposals should be beneficial to children of all age groups.

governments reintroduced and extended the tax deductions for children, but monthly maternity benefits have not increased. The federal government programme for maternity leave is complemented by some of the German states (Länder) with a conservative government. In line with conservative view on the role of the mother, "A basic condition for additional support [by these Länder programmes] is a withdrawal from the labour market" (Zimmermann 1993:210).

Similar to in The Netherlands the German compensation of earnings during pregnancy/delivery leave is high: 100% of earnings during two months ('Mutterschutz'). Thereafter, and for non-working women also till the child is two months old, a flat rate is paid of DM 600 per month. However, from the 7th month onwards, the flat rate is means tested against family income.[13]

Fully in line with the character of the Esping-andersen's second type of welfare state, child care facilities in Germany are mainly provided by local governments and by churches and other welfare organisations. Child care centres are subsidised, resulting in a low average monthly user's price of about DM 65 in 1987. Daycare and commercial facilities charge higher prices. There are no subsidies for non-institutional child care. Child care expenses are not tax deductible.

Sweden

Sweden is the prototype of the social democratic welfare state with a long history of public involvement and expenditure in provision of facilities to combine work and family responsibilities, like long job protection with high compensation and subsidised full day care for children as a social service available for everyone. Swedish parental leaves replaced 90% of lost earnings during 15 months until 1996. From 1st of January 1996, 75% of earnings is paid during 10 months and two months are set aside so that the father gets 90% of his salary if he chooses to be on child care leave and the mother gets 90% of her salary if she chooses to be on leave. This rule was instituted in order to give fathers an incentive to take at least one month of leave. If he does not 75% of the mother's salary applies to eleven months and 90% of the mother's salary to one month. Thereafter a flat rate

---

[13]   There are no figures on the%age of working mothers that are eligible to the DM 600 pm from the 7th month after childbearing.

will be paid during 3 months. Non-working wives receive this flat rate during the entire 18 months.

The Swedish policy has been to supply full daycare for children after their first birth day till the age of 7, when they go to primary school, in the vicinity of the child's home, so that children can see their friends at weekends and parents are not tied to a particular employer who provides child care. This is the opposite of Dutch policies that make employees tied to a particular employer. Swedish municipalities have a right to taxation, and a large share of the Swedish population pays only the municipal proportional income tax. Revenues from the municipal tax finance between 40-50% of the total cost of day care for children. The fees Swedish parents pay for public day care (mostly income dependent) averaged less than 10% of total costs for the whole period 1975-1990 (Gustafsson and Stafford, 1992). In 1994 the fees had increased to 13.4% (Socialstyrelsen, 1995).

During the 1970s Swedish employees were granted 10 days per year of paid leave for sick children (1975, extended to 90 days per year in 1988) and 180 days (3 months paid, 3 months flat rate) for additional care till the child is 8 years old (1978). In addition all parents who were full time employed were given the legal right to reduce work hours at own cost to 75% till the child is 8 (1979).

The main Swedish retrenchment measures in the 1990s resulting in for example the reduction of the earnings related parental benefits, represented deeper cuts than those undertaken by the neo-liberal governments in the other three countries. In this respect Swedish policy makers appear more resolute in their efforts to cope with the economic crisis than policy makers in the other countries. However these measures are propagated as temporary necessary sacrifices and not as a move into a more residualist direction, still Sweden is spending more than any of the other countries on family policies. The downsizing aimed to maintain four aspects of Swedish social provision: universal public services, basic security reflected in "citizen" benefits, income security provided by earnings related benefits, and minimal reliance on means tested benefits. The Social Democrats decided to cut universal child allowances rather than make them means tested. In the election campaign of 1998, social democrats have proposed a low universal maximum day care fee for parents, which if implemented would increase the day care subsidy substantially again.

Conclusion

According to the Esping-Andersen's welfare state typology, public involvement in subsidising family's cost of children is strong in Germany and Sweden. However, the ideology behind the governmental policies on the family is different in Germany and Sweden, whereas Swedish policies aim at facilitating the combination of work and family in guaranteeing job protection, generously paid caring time till the child's first anniversary and subsidised full day care thereafter, German policies subsidise the family financially by benefiting the primary and only earner with high allowances for a non working spouse and children, and offer a long job protected period to the mother without earnings incentives, to care for the child in combination with subsidised part day play schools.

Public expenses on cost of children were quite low in The Netherlands until 1990s and particularly in the United Kingdom. Since the 1960s Dutch women's labour force participation rates were the lowest of all four countries which meant that very few women were entitled to benefits as workers. As most women cared for their own children, public subsidies for childcare (part day play schools) were granted only gradually. However, since the 1990s Dutch policies aim at women's labour force participation, and equal role sharing in paid and unpaid work including child care. Public expenditures stimulate employers to rent child care places for their employees. Furthermore the employees' legal right to reduce work hours and increase work hours again is on the political agenda to encourage equal role sharing within households. The ideology of British social policies has been to provide minimum facilities for parents. Cost of children are parents' private responsibility. If earnings are very low women can make use of child care spaces for free.

Social Policy Ideologies 2: principle of maintenance and care

Does massive state intervention in welfare provision automatically benefit most people, including women?

In a publication edited by Sainsbury (1994) a number of feminist scholars depart from the Esping-andersen (1990) typology of welfare states in order to show that the gender perspective is absent from this typology.[14]

---

[14]   Esping-Andersen (1996) admits his lack of gender perspective in earlier work and emphasizes gender and also supply and price of services.

Sainsbury (1994, 1996) argues that sharp divergences in women's and social rights in welfare states are not revealed by mainstream welfare state typologies, since they distinguish between three bases of entitlements for welfare benefits: need, market work performance and citizenship. An alternative typology is forwarded which emphasises the extent to which social policies are organised according to the idea that the man is the breadwinner, based on two other bases of entitlement, the principle of maintenance and care. Sainsbury isolates dimensions of variation related to gender in order to examine the interaction between these dimensions and the welfare state variations designated as important by mainstream analysts.

The most important result is the distinction between the breadwinner as against the individual typology in social policy, presented in Table 2.2. As with all typologies the breadwinner typology does not totally coincide with some existing set of policies.

The prevalent familial ideology at the end of the 1960s in Germany, Sweden, The Netherlands and the United Kingdom, as reflected in legislation, applauded a breadwinner model: a traditional division of labour with the husband as the primary earner and the wife as the carer.

Sweden

Swedish policies diverged from those of the other countries in significant ways. First, as a result of social rights based on citizenship, the privileged status of the breadwinner was not translated into social legislation to the same extent as in the other three countries. This basis of eligibility resulted in uniform and personal entitlement within marriage. Married women had individual rights to a basic old age pension, disability and sickness benefits, and these rights were unaffected by marital status.

By contrast, the basis of entitlement to social benefits of married women and men in the other countries was highly differentiated. Married women's entitlement was largely derived from their husbands rights, and they lacked individual entitlement. Secondly, married women's entitlements were enhanced by the gradual demise of means tested benefits, e.g. the 1946 pension reform that made citizen pensions the main form of old age provision, the 1948 introduction of universal child allowances, the 1955 conversion of means tested maternity allowances into flat rate maternity grants. Thirdly, legislation has highlighted the needs of children resulting in supplements for children instead of for wives. Fourthly, the principle of care has strengthened women's claims to benefits both as mothers and caregivers rather than as wives. The Swedish policy reforms in the 1930s introduced maternity benefits that compensated for the costs of motherhood rather than for the loss of earned income. Similarly child allowances were paid to all mothers. This Swedish system of allowances together with sickness cash benefits were the first benefits explicitly recognising work in the home as a basis of entitlement.

Table 2.2: The Breadwinner and the Individual Model of Social Policy

Dimension	Breadwinner	Individual model
Family ideology	Strict division of labour	Shared roles
	Husband = earner	Husband = earner/carer
	Wife = carer	Wife = earner/carer
Entitlement	Differentiated among spouses	Uniform
Basis of entitlement	Breadwinner	Other
Recipient of benefits	Head of household	Individual
Unit of benefit	Household or family	Individual
Unit of contributions	Household	Individual
Taxation	Joint taxation	Separate taxation
	Deductions for dependents	Equal tax relief
Employment and wage policies	Priority to men	Aimed at both sexes
Sphere of care	Primarily private	Strong state involvement
Caring work	Unpaid	Paid component

Source: Sainsbury (1994)

The allowances put unpaid work in the home on a par with paid work outside the home, but benefit levels indicate that paid work was more highly valued. Since the mid 1950s benefit levels related to work outside the home have outstripped those of a mother without paid work. The growing gap should not obscure the important fact that the benefits of the non-working Swedish mother have been generally higher than those of working mothers receiving maternity benefits in the other three countries. As the period of leave lengthened from three months in the mid-1950s to eighteen months in the 1990s, parental benefits can be interpreted as compensation for care in the home or paid care work. This interpretation and the fact that mainly women use the long parental leave[15] shows that mainly women do use legal job protection without refreshing labour market capabilities, and therefore the individual model is not yet an equal role sharing model. Similarly, the right to cut work hours to 30 hours per week

---

[15]   In 1988 roughly 90% of Swedish children under the age of one were exclusively cared for by their parents (mothers) who were on paid parental leave (SCB 1989). For older pre-school children, 1 to 6 years old, the per cent cared for exclusively by parents fell to 30%.

until the child is 8, and the right to increase work hours again thereafter is for one of the parents, usually the mother.

However, already in 1974 Swedish fathers became eligible to take leave and since then Sweden conducted campaigns to encourage fathers to make greater use of parental benefits. There has been some response. In Sweden all fathers used 7.5% of total days replaced in 1987, which is a slight increase from 4.3% in 1978, and 24.5% of all fathers received some benefits, a rise from 20.4% in 1978. Swedish fathers who received benefits were on leave for 29.3 days on average in 1987, compared to only 10.9 days in 1978 (National Insurance Board, 1989). Among married and employed parents, fathers who used any benefits were on leave for 43 days on average (National Insurance Board, 1990). The willingness of married and employed Swedish fathers to take out any parental leave was found to depend more on the size of their wives' earnings than on their own. The higher the pay of the mother, the larger the proportion of fathers who received benefits, regardless of the fathers' earnings (Sundström & Stafford, 1994). The parental leave program in 1996 includes one month, which if used by the father replaces 90%of his earnings, the so called 'daddy month'.

The Swedish tax system has totally individual tax scales since 1971, which do not pay any attention to the number of dependents. As a result, the small incomes of part-time working wives are taxed at lower tax rates than the large incomes of full-time working husbands in Sweden. This aspect of the tax systems implies that Swedish wives have an economic incentive to increase work hours relative to their husbands, and a part-time job contributes relatively more to family income.

The Netherlands

In contrast to Swedish benefits, Dutch benefits were almost entirely attached to the principle of maintenance in 1970,[16] even family allowances and child delivery were covered through the father's insurance. There were no maternity grants or benefits for non-working mothers or for mothers who were self-employed or family workers.

---

[16] The principle of maintenance implied that benefits and wages themselves had to be adequate to meet the needs of the average family. In 1947 men=s wages changed from individual to breadwinner standard. Married women became deprived of individual entitlement as long as the family was intact.

However during the 1980s and 1990s[17] coverage was extended through the individualisation of entitlement to benefits due to unemployment, sickness (including pregnancy). Child allowances are universal benefits and awarded to the mother in 1996.

Dutch taxation system is individual however there is an adults transferable deduction.[18] Bekkering, Grift and Siegers (1986), Bruyn-Hundt and Van der Linden (1989) and Vlasblom (1998) find only a small influence from the taxation system on women's labour supply in The Netherlands.

Dutch public policies aim at increasing women's labour force participation and equal sharing of paid and unpaid work of household members. The Netherlands is the most part time working country among all countries we have statistics for, certainly among OECD countries. However the labour force participation of women in the age category 25-54 is still fairly low in comparison with younger Dutch women and Dutch men in the age category 25-34. Since most women leave the labour market after child bearing the public policies aim at labour force attachment of young mothers.

Since 1990 there is a legal right to 6 months part time parental leave per parent, which makes the total leave period per child quite large (12 months per child). Among all mothers 41% take parental leaves. Among mothers working in the public sector 58% take parental leave (which is paid) and among mothers working in the private sector 24% do. Only 10% of fathers take parental leave: 35% of fathers in the public sector (paid) and 8% of fathers in the private sector (SCP, 1997:119).

Days off for the father are granted by 94% of CAO's of which 83% offer 2 days, intended as one day to attend delivery of the child and one day to register the child. From 1991 till 1996 the percentage of CAO's offering more than 2 days off for fathers increased from 4.1 to 11.3.

The Dutch government sees the relationship between employers and employees as the instrument to attain equal role sharing in paid work and unpaid work, including payment of parental leave. There are fiscal

---

[17]   For an overview of the recent and historical public debates on work and family in The Netherlands see Cuyvers, P., K. de Hoog & H. Pott-Buter (1997).

[18]   One argument against the individual model in the Dutch debate on taxation is that similar gross income leaves a two earner household more than a one earner household. But the counter argument is that buying services that replace the unpaid work and child care of a housewife has to be paid out of net income. Housewives' work is not liable to taxation.

incentives for employers to create child care facilities for their employees, and fiscal facilities for employees who use this childcare.[19] However, the contribution of parents to meet child care costs (formally organised by their employer) is based on total family after tax earnings.[20]

Germany

The German public policy on the family developed from the 1960s till present further in a breadwinner direction. The German tax system is mostly breadwinner oriented, since joint taxation encourages the second earner to specialise in home production as soon as there are differences in the earnings potential of both spouses. The small incomes of part-time working wives are added to the large incomes of full-time working husbands and taxed at his marginal tax rate. Gustafsson (1992) finds that the contribution to family income of the secondary earner under German taxation is smaller after tax than it is before tax.

The parental leave period has been extended from 10 months in 1986 to 36 months job protection in 1993. However benefits are kept low, the benefit rate for each of the 6 months was DM 600. From the 7th month on

---

[19]   Groot and Maassen van den Brink (1996) point at two risks. First, child care will be supplied by firms with female dominated personnel registers. The financing of child care will be out of the 'possible wage increase for employees'. There is a risk that the wage differentials between men and women will increase when female dominated firms and female dominated sectors have less wage increase than other firms and sectors, and might be seen as unlawful wage discrimination of the female sex. Secondly employers might be more willing to invest in child care for highly educated employees because it is more costly to replace them. This would be a disadvantage for low educated employees who are also in need for child care. Maassen van den Brink and Groot (1995) already showed that mainly highly educated parents use formal child care facilities. Women making use of formal child care for their children earn 1,5 to 2 times as much compared to women who use play schools and informal child care.

[20]   The following case shows the costs and benefits analysis of labour force participation and child care in The Netherlands. A couple consists of full-time workers, one spouse (the female) earns slightly less than the other. The female spouse decides to take unpaid leave half time after the pregnancy leave: which leaves net earnings a bit more than half of her full-time net earnings. However, parents= contribution in the costs of part-time child care needed, then, (subsidized by her employer or not), depends on net family earnings. If the woman refrains from paid work, the men pays less taxation because of the transferable adult=s allowance. The couple becomes eligible to a subsidy for housing. In addition the housewife is insured (by the breadwinner) for costs related to sickness by paying only a very small amount. On the basis of this calculation the couple will probably decide that it is not beneficial for the second earner to participate in market work (Ministry of Social Affairs, September 1997).

the benefit for each child depended on annual net family income two years before birth and was reduced on a sliding scale basis. The benefit period was extended to 24 months in 1993. In 1994 an upper income limit on the receipt of benefits in the first 6th months was introduced. The upper limit is DM 100,000. German fathers, have a right to take parental leave, but during 1986-1988 only 0.6% of all fathers in Germany made use of their right, 1.4% of all fathers received the parental benefits (Deutscher Bundestag 1990).

Since child care facilities are meant to educate the children, not to facilitate the combination of paid work and children for parents, they accept children older than 3, part day and not during lunch (2 hours). Similarly schools are open 5 hours a day and assume a parent to help with the home work. Zimmermann (1993: 215) mentions the conviction of many social groups in Germany that only the mother can provide adequate care for babies, which means that the unwillingness of the government to provide institutional care for very young children assumes mainly mothers who care for the child till the age of 3, and part time thereafter. In addition, part-time jobs are rarely available (Vlasblom, 1998) and there are no public policies that aim at part-time work.

United Kingdom

At first glance the United Kingdom seems to fit the breadwinner model less well than The Netherlands and Germany. Payment of family allowances was made to the mother, which can be interpreted as an initial recognition of the principle of care. Secondly medical care through the National Health Service was a citizen benefit unaffected by family status, whereas Dutch and German married women were covered as family members. Thirdly, British women received a more generous tax allowance. Fourthly, the unit of benefit was the individual not the family. As a beneficiary the husband received an adult dependant allowance when his wife was not in paid work, and his wife was entitled to a dependant's pension without extra contributions when she reached retirement age.

Nonetheless, underlying similarities in both the United Kingdom, The Netherlands and former West Germany were that the husband was the prime recipient of benefits, the wife's benefits were derived from her husband's social rights, and the tax systems treated the husband as family provider generously. The British national insurance scheme allowed married women to choose not to pay full contributions and instead rely upon husband's contributions, but in the process they forfeited their claim to benefits in their own right. In the 1970s three quarters of married women in Britain had opted out of the national insurance scheme (Land, 1985). Married women who remained in the British national insurance scheme and paid full contributions, received lower benefits than married men and single persons unless they were the main bread winner (Groves 1983). The adult dependent allowances was only paid for dependents without an income or with earnings less than the allowance. Furthermore married women were not allowed to claim child additions. In married couples only the husband could apply for means tested assistance.

In 1991 the Britain adopted individual taxation. However a transferable Zero Rate Allowance (ZRA) remained, that together with steep progressive tax rates create a disincentive for British secondary earners (women) to work. This effect is larger with increasing amounts of ZRA, but once in the labour market the separate tax system creates an incentive for women to work longer paid hours. The relatively large personal non-transferable ZRA in the British tax system generates an incentive for married women to work part time.

Conclusion

From the breadwinner model in the 1960s Sweden has changed towards the individual model fairly soon. In contrast to Sweden, Germany developed further in the breadwinner direction. The social policies in The Netherlands that were the most breadwinner oriented in the 1960s have developed from the late 1980s and 1990s towards an individual direction, with explicit public encouragement of equal role sharing within households. The social policies in the United Kingdom are in between the breadwinner and the individual model.

Actual public policies on the family

In Table 2.3 actual family policies are summarised. Women's labour market behaviour in the period they (time to) have children will depend financially on her earnings (and earnings related benefits), her partner's earnings and the availability of affordable care for the child by some other person.

Already before children are born, earnings of household members are affected by social policies, as regards whether the taxation system benefits the primary earner in the household at the cost of the secondary earner, or not. The German tax system is mostly breadwinner oriented, and encourages the second earner to specialise in home production as soon as there are differences in the earnings potential of both spouses. The Swedish tax system on the other hand, has totally individual tax scales, which implies that Swedish wives have more economic incentive to increase work hours relative to their husbands than German wives, and a part-time job contributes relatively more to family income. The British and Dutch tax system are individual but have a transferable allowance. Secondly, income related maternity benefits might result in higher (full-time) employment rates before child bearing.

After childbearing parent's earnings (per hour) after taxes and social premium contributions are traded off against the child care cost (per hour) by a third person. Since not many couples prefer both spouses to work full-time when their children are born, the availability of part time jobs and the treatment of part-time jobs in taxation and social premiums contributions, are important. Public policies lowering social security payments for small part time jobs relatively to long part time jobs make small part time jobs financially more attractive. For German and British employers social security payments are dependent on earnings per week. In Sweden all contributions have to be paid by the employers as a flat rate on the sum of wages. The Swedish wage bill tax is therefore neutral between hours of work, but also larger, which creates a larger wedge between supply price and demand price of labour.

Social policies which aim at the combination of work and child care, offer earnings related benefits during leave, job protection, and make child care affordable and available for children of all age groups. We expect that a short job protection period (in the United Kingdom and The Netherlands) and/or a small parental leave benefit (in Germany, the United Kingdom and The Netherlands (if employed in the private sector)) might induce some mothers to reenter the labour force earlier than mothers who can rely on better provisions. After child birth, the earnings related compensation is paid to German women during two months (100% of earnings), to Dutch women during 2,5-3 months (100% of earnings), to British mothers during 1,5 months (90% of earnings) and to Swedish mothers during 11-12 months (75% of earnings since 1996). The job protection period after birth is for German women 36 months, for Dutch women (10-12 weeks (pregnancy leave after child birth) plus 6 months part time parental leave: 8,5-9 months), for British mothers 7 months (29 weeks) and for Swedish mothers 18 months. Some British, Dutch and German mothers, may for economic reasons return to work when the child is half a year old or even younger.

Table 2.3: Actual Policies Relevant to Work for Recent Mothers in Germany, The Netherlands, The United Kingdom and Sweden

	West Germany	The Netherlands	United Kingdom	Sweden
Taxation Regime				
Basic allowance	Splitting tariff since 1948	individual since 1973	Individual since 1991	Individual since 1971
Adults transferable pa	Yes	Yes	Yes	No
	1992: DM 5616	1997: f 7102 ± DM 6230	1994: £ 1720 [b] ± DM 3800	1995:10000 SEK± DM2200
Adults non transf. Pa	No		1994: £ 3445 [b] ± DM 3445	
			No [c]	No [d]
Child allowance pa, pch	1992: DM 4104 [a] Freibetrag für Kinderbetreuungskosten 1992: 1st child max. :DM 4000 2nd child max. DM 2000	1997: f 5682 ± DM 4971		
Social security payments employee/employer:	0-100% if earnings< DM 610 pm; else 50-50% [c]	50-50%	0-0% if earnings< £ 52 pw ± DM 494 pm ; else 50-50 [c]	0-100% (flat rate on sum of wages) [c]
Child benefits paid to: (pm, pch)	carer [e]: 1996:DM 200 1st+2nd, DM 300 3rd+[b] Zusatzkindergeld (1992: DM 65 pm) for (low) income earners[a]	mother 1998: f 316/3m ± DM 93/m 1st f 384/3m ± DM 112/m 2nd f 452/3m ± DM 132/m 3rd	mother 1994: £ 10 pw ± DM 90/m 1st £ 8 pw ± DM 70/m 2nd+[b]	mother 1989: 9000 SEK pa ± DM 170/m all children [i]

Pregnancy benefits				
% of earnings	100% (Mutterschaftsgeld)	100%	90%: (6 wks); ± 20% (12 wks); £ 30 pw ± DM 285 pm f) thereafter 0	Since 1996
Total period	14 wks / 6 wks 'prebirth'	16 wks / 4 to 6 wks 'prebirth'	40 wks / max 29 wks 'postbirth'	
Parental benefits pch				
% of earnings	75% public sector, else 0			75%, 1 month pp 90%
During (mths)	6 pp			12 per family
Flat rate (pm)	DM 600 (Erziehungsgeld) > 7th mth means tested a)			SEK 60 pd; ±DM 400
Total period paid (mths)	1993: 24	6 pp:12 public sector only		15
Total period 'post birth' (mths)	1992: 24 b), 1993:36	6 pp:12		18 d)
Right to share between parents?	Yes	Each parent own right		Yes
if subsequent child fast?	Same benefits for subseq.	n.a.		'speed premium':2nd birth within 30 mths after 1st,% based on earnings befr 1st birth
Eligibility criteria for job protection	No	Minimum 1 year employed	insurance period: 2 yrs>16 hrs pw or 5 yrs, 8-16 hrs pw f); since 1995 no hrs conditions	6 mths before delivery, or 12 of 24 mths before delivery
Right to working hours	< 20 hrs pw b) if on parental leave	>= 20 hrs pw for 6 months (child<8); for both parents	no	Right to 6 hrs pd (child<8) for 1 parent

Paid occasional care	10-25 days per parent depends on number of children (age < 12)[b]	No 1 or 2 days	no	120 days pa pch (age < 12): 14 dys: 80% of earnings; >14 dys 90% of earnings[d]
Childcare	Public part day Children 3 yrs+ no care during lunch (2 hrs)	Private and market 1990s: subsidies all ages	private and market	Public full day Pre school integrated in day care centers but extra available for children not in day care[k]
Priority to working mothers	Yes, single mothers priority	Yes	Yes	Yes[d]
School				
Start: child's age	6	4	5	7 since 1994, upon parents' choice, from age 6
Schoolday	5 hrs pd; over at 1 p.m.; differs between schools[a]	Differs between age groups. Sometimes provisions for children to stay during lunch, and after school care	Approx. 9 a.m-3 p.m. Local policies: Ages 4-5 admitted to infant classes in primary schools; Age 3: ft/pt nursery education	Uniform, includes all school work and lunch.[d] 1994: 50% of children 7-10 in subs. after schoolcare[k]

Pch=per child; pp=per parent; Pa= per annum; pm= per month; pw=per week; pd= per day; mth(s) =months; a) Zimmermann (1993), b) Ditch et al. (1995); c) Vermeulen et al. (1995); d) Gustafsson & Stafford (1995) e) Übersicht über die Soziale Sicherheit (1991); f) Dex et al. (1993); g) McRae (1991); h) Ostner (1993); i)Aronsson and Walker (1995); j) Moss (1988, 1990); k) Socialstyrelsen (1995); l) Cohen and Clarke 1986:77; m) Brown and Small (1991), Daniel (1990);n) Groot and Maassen van den Brink (1996); o) Kindercentra, CBS (1991) p) Mutsaers (1997)

After a while of fulltime caring and after the job protection period expires the combination of care and market work is the desired status for many women. After the child's first birthday Swedish mothers are likely to have left the status of fulltime caring and taken a job, assisted by subsidised day care for the child. In the other countries the age of children admitted in full day care, and the availability and price of spaces is less aimed at assisting a mother with paid work. Waiting lists for child care and 84% of mothers making use of informal care, show that formal care in The Netherlands is not fully arranged yet. Also the hours spent in day care differs between countries. Dutch children on average spend less than 3 days per week in a child care centre,[21] whereas it is more common for Swedish children when they are 18 months and older to be 5 days in day care. Like Dutch and German mothers who mostly rely on part time Kindergarten, most British mothers have been compelled to rely on ad hoc arrangements and the informal sector is dominant in this respect, though there is a minority of women in full-time jobs with an employed partner, making a substantial cash investment in childminders, nannies or nurseries (Ward, Dale and Joshi, 1996).

Women's timing of having the first child and subsequent children is also expected to be affected by government policies on the family. Career oriented women who face difficulties in combining work and children are expected to have their first child later (or refrain from having children) than career oriented women who can make use of public policies that enable women to have time to organise a career and a child. Also earnings related maternity benefits like in Sweden are expected to induce women to have high earnings before maternity, especially if there is a 'speed premium'. The Swedish 'speed premium', entitles a Swedish mother who gives birth to a second child within 30 months of the first birth, to have her income compensation for the second child's parental leave period computed on the basis of her earnings before the first child was born. This allows women to work part time or if their employer agrees to extend the leave period not working at all between births and have substantial income during the leave period for the second child. Women with lower payment who face high child care costs and little career prospects may leave the labour market after

---

[21]   In 1991 the average number of hours per week spent in a in child care centre were 16.3, in 1995 this number had increased to 17.9 (Maassen van den Brink and Groot, 1996).

the birth of their first child, but might postpone maternity to minimise life-time earnings loss.

Conclusions

First, we classified governmental policies on the family in Germany, Sweden, The Netherlands and the United Kingdom inspired by Esping-andersen's mainstream welfare state typology. According to the degree of public involvement and the dependence of eligibility to benefits on labour market performance, in the family policy area, the United Kingdom is classified as a liberal welfare state, The Netherlands and Germany as Christian democratic welfare states and Sweden as a social democratic welfare state. Secondly, Sainsbury's typology helped to characterise the family policy areas according to their male breadwinner orientation, and how the degree of breadwinner orientation changed from the 1960s till present day. Whereas there are elements of the breadwinner model and the individual model in all countries it is safe to say that the breadwinner model is now more evident in Germany and the individual model is more evident in Sweden. The Netherlands and the United Kingdom occupy a place in between on the breadwinner individual axis.

Germany offers tax-benefits to one earner/one carer couples, a long maternity leave period with low pay, part-time child care facilities and part-time school day. Sweden on the other hand, has individual taxation, a long well paid parental leave period, full-day subsidised child care for children of all age groups, leave to care for sick children and schooldays including lunch and substantial after school care. The Christian Democratic influence in Dutch government policy on the family has been strong for a long period, but the political climate changed towards a more individual direction during the last decade. Dutch public involvement in the provision of child care increased during the 1990s. In line with the Dutch view on the state as being an agent in harmonising the conflicting interests of groups with the aim of maintaining their autonomy, the government stimulates social partners (employers and employees) to invest and fund jointly child care facilities. The United Kingdom adopted a system of individual taxation in 1991 (more similar to the individual model) but utilises one transferable basic deduction which is an element of joint taxation (more similar to the breadwinner model). In addition the United Kingdom has limited social security rights for married women since the benefits depend on husband's income (Sainsbury 1994) which is also more similar to the breadwinner model. Since public involvement in family policies in the United Kingdom is the weakest of the four countries, the United Kingdom must be seen as a liberal welfare state, whereas Germany, The Netherlands and Sweden are best compared on the breadwinner-individual model axis.

Having clarified the nature of welfare state variations and the way in which public policies on the combination of work and children in the countries included in this study differ, we turn to the empirical analyses in chapters 4-7.

3 Creating Comparative Fertility and Work Files from Household Panel Data Sets

Introduction

This chapter describes the construction of comparative 'fertility and work' files from household panel data sets for the purpose of analysing women's labour force transitions in connection with childbirth, wife's contribution to family' earnings around childbirth, the connection between paid careers and the timing and spacing of births, and the optimal age of maternity.

The following variables are requested. First, we need information on birth events in a woman's life per year and month, distinguished by birth order. Secondly, we need information on labour market participation and changes in labour market participation of women around the time of child birth on a monthly basis. Thirdly, we want to take into account the human capital and earnings of the spouse of the selected women, which means that we have to find out whom the selected mother is living with at the time of child birth. Fourthly, we need information on the human capital of the woman and of her spouse at the time they have a child. Fifthly, we need information on the price they get for their human capital in the market, i.e. their market wages ideally measured at the time of having a child, and at specific points in time before and after the birth of a child.

To analyse these themes in a comparative perspective we use for Germany the German Socio Economic (SozioÖkonomische) Panel (GSOEP, Wagner et al.(1991)). For the United Kingdom we use the British Household Panel Study (BHPS, Taylor (1992)). For The Netherlands we use the Arbeidsaanbodpanel (labour supply panel) collected by Organisatie voor Strategisch Arbeidsmarktonderzoek (OSA, Allaart et al (1987)), and for Sweden we use the HUShällens ekonomiska levnadsförhällanden(HUS, Klevmarken and Olovsson (1993), Flood et al.(1996)).'Household panel data sets' in this study refer only to the household panel data   sets included in this study (GSOEP, BHPS, OSA and HUS). One of the aims of the household panel data collections is to gain insight into the functioning of the supply side of the labour market, by connecting information on individual supply of labour of household members. The panel-character of the data sets, means that the initial representative sample of the country's household population has been followed over time. Households are dropped e.g. when all household members have reached age 65, or if all household members refuse to participate. Such households have been replaced in a manner that each wave provides a cross sectional representation of the national population of households.[22]

However, the household panel data sets are not totally similar across countries, even if we only work with the sections on the labour market position and the household composition. Furthermore, the data sets have different degrees of standardisation over time because in some countries new research topics emerge that replace old by new requested information. However, by carefully comparing the data sets we have been able to construct a comparative data set suited to analyse empirically our research interests. One important feature of the household panel data sets is the 'event' character of the fertility and labour market histories, on a monthly basis.

This chapter is organised as follows. Section 3.2 describes the contents of each national household panel data set and discusses its advantages and limits for our research purposes. Section 3.3 deals with the identification of birth events in a woman's life and the construction of women's labour market events around childbirth. Section 3.4 deals with finding in the data sets the husbands or cohabiting men with whom the selected mother is living at the time of giving birth to children. Section 3.5 discusses our use of labour market histories around births. Section 3.6 pays attention to the measurement of earnings around the time of having children. Section 3.7 shows the cross country comparability of educational level and section 3.8 gives details on the construction of a variable on work experience of women and their spouses at the time of having children. Section 3.9 presents conclusions.

---

[22]   For example, OSA uses the random walk method for replacement of households, variables for selection are sex, age, family size and region. It is requested that all household members of the newly selected household participate in the interview, otherwise the household is considered as non responding, and a new household is recruited.

Description of household panel data sets

We label the household panel data set of a country 'survey', and we label each year in which the data is collected in a survey 'wave'. The request of information itself is labelled 'interview'. Each survey is organised on a household level and on household members level, which we label 'personal level'.

Each survey consists of three types of data as regards the time period they cover. First, in each wave information is requested on (the calendar year prior to) the year in which the interview is held, e.g. monthly earnings. Secondly, additional 'spell data' are collected requesting information on specific topics, e.g. changes in household composition, labour market position in the period between waves. Finally, retrospective data are collected on for example fertility history and labour market history over the period before a person participated in the survey.

Special features of samples in the surveys in this study The German survey, GSOEP, has a typical design in that the initial population is divided into two separate samples. Sample A: People in private households in the western states of Germany in 1984, where the head of the household was not of Turkish, Greek, Yugoslavian, Spanish or Italian nationality. Foreign persons of other nationalities are included in this sample but they make up an insignificant portion of the population of 1984. The second sample, Sample B, consists of people in private households in the western states of Germany in 1984, where the head of the household was of Turkish, Greek, Yugoslavian, Spanish or Italian nationality.[23] The variables have been collected identically between sample A and B because the purpose of the collection design is to compare Germans and foreigners.[24] A new sample of immigrants called sample D, collected from 1994 onwards, includes immigrants who came to the western states of Germany from 1984

---

[23] Sample B oversamples these five numerically largest foreign nationality groups ('guestworkers' recruited from the late 1950s till 1973). Sample B consists of five autonomous samples: 400 Turkish, 300 Yugoslav, 300 Italian, 200 Greek and 200 Spanish households.The sampled households and all their members are followed as long as they stay in Germany. Once included in the sample B a person remains in this sample even if (s)he changes to German nationality.

[24] There are also specific questions on foreigners like whether other family members will immigrate, the respondents's willingness to return to the native country, language competence, ethnic orientation and whether they integrate in German society: have German friends, relationships.

onwards, excluding migrants from East to West Germany after reunification. In the British, Dutch, and Swedish surveys immigrants are included if they are selected by the general sample criteria. Furthermore, persons who do not speak Swedish/Dutch well enough for an interview, are excluded from HUS/OSA respectively. For most purposes this makes it impossible to study immigrants specifically in the British, Dutch and Swedish samples. In 1990, immediately after unification, a sample on former Eastern Germany including migrants from former East to former West Germany, sample C, was added. The analyses laid down in Chapters 4-7 cover Germany during 1984-1992. We have worked with sample A, B en C (only the period 1990-92) in the analyses of labour force transitions in connection with child birth and with only sample A in the other analyses.

The Dutch OSA labour supply survey[25] has a more narrow scope aiming at the labour market,[26] as compared to the GSOEP, BHPS and HUS surveys which also aim at covering housing, health and consumption issues for example. However, the OSA survey provides data on changes in household composition including childbirth and changes in labour market position on a monthly basis comparable to the other countries.

The first Swedish household panel survey HUS, has added relatively large additional samples in 1986, 1993 and 1996 to increase total sample size.[27] Furthermore the HUS team made large efforts to include again

---

[25]   OSA also conducts a labour demand panel, a representative data set of Dutch organizations covering employer/employees issues. When OSA is mentioned in this study, this refers to the OSA labour supply survey.

[26]   The important motive to start the OSA supply panel survey was the level of unemployment in the early eighties. The OSA sample is a representative sample of the potential Dutch labour force with specific information on unemployed and women who are out of the labour force. Praat & Mekkelholt (1991) point at over sampling of women, under sampling of unemployed persons and over sampling of long time unemployed within the unemployed group. However, they conclude that these sampling problems are not severe enough to endanger the OSA as a reasonable representation of the Dutch supply side of the labour market. In any case we do not think that our analyses of a group of relatively young Dutch women will suffer from these sampling problems.

[27]   We profit from the additional HUS sample in 1993 consisting of 1643 individuals, 507 women in the age category 18-45 of whom 122 women have had their first birth during 1984-1993, and of whom 96 have had a second birth during 1984-1993, and of whom 44 have had a third birth during 1984-1993. If we consider the period 1991 to 1993 45 women in this additional sample have had their first child, 35 women have given birth to their second child and 12 women have given birth to their third child. The 1996
[continued on next page]

'drop-outs' over the period 1984-1993 in 1993 and 'drop-outs' over the period 1993-1996, in 1996 (in separate files 'Bortfallundersökningen'). They also collected monthly spell information on labour market changes from the entry interview till the last wave of the panel for these former drop-outs. However, monthly spell information on changes in the hours of work per week has not been collected for this group of 'drop outs'. This means that it is not possible to distinguish between full time and part time work, which complicates the update of employment experience till date of birth of children in these samples.

A complication of HUS for our purposes is that waves differ over time. First, the waves in 1988 and 1991 were much smaller in the requested information. Secondly, the wave in 1988 included only individuals who participated in 1986, and the wave in 1991 included the respondents from 1988 and new members to the old household, whereas all other waves also included new households. Thirdly, some requests were not standardised across waves, which we will see in the following sections.

Observation periods, frequencies of data collection and sample sizes

In Table 3.1 we present the observation period, the frequency of data collection and the sample size of each survey. The surveys in West Germany (GSOEP), Sweden (HUS) and The Netherlands (OSA) start around the same year, namely the former two in 1984 and the latter in 1985. The survey in Great Britain (BHPS) starts later, in 1991. We make use of the waves in Germany and Great Britain till 1992, and for Sweden and The Netherlands we use waves up to and including 1996. The 1992 wave in BHPS, and the 1985 wave in OSA, collected retrospective information on a monthly basis concerning fertility and labour market behaviour on the period before the initial wave. We can therefore cover Great Britain and The Netherlands for a period of more than 10 years, 1980-1992 for Britain and 1980-1996 for The Netherlands, of which 1980-1985 retrospectively.

The frequency of data collection differs between surveys. GSOEP and BHPS are annual surveys, whereas OSA is a bi-annual survey from 1986 onwards, and HUS is mostly bi-annual but tri-annual between 1988-1991 and 1993-1996. First, the frequency in data collection is important for

wave adds the "after birth" observation on labor market status and earnings for births in the period 1993-1996.

the frequency of information that is only collected for the year in which the interview takes place e.g. earnings data in 1984, 1985, etc, or earnings data in 1984, 1986, 1988, 1991 etc. Secondly, as a consequence, the length of the time period that needs to be covered by 'spell data', differs with frequency. Spell data cover a one year period in Germany and Britain, a two year period in The Netherlands and a two or three year period in Sweden. The reliability of the spell data will not differ much according to the length of the period, but for our analyses it means that frequency together with attrition is important for the number of observations we include in our analyses. For example, the GSOEP annual survey implies that a German woman has to give retrospective information for 12 months. If she does not participate in one survey we lose information on the previous 12 months. The HUS surveys are two or three years apart. Each subsequent time that a Swedish woman participates in the HUS survey, we have labour market information on a monthly basis for two or three years. If she does not participate in a subsequent survey we lose information on two or three years.

The spell data on changes in household composition and labour market status between waves in each survey are rather standardised over time. There are two exceptions. OSA is detailed in the collection of the changes in labour force status but is the least standardised across waves compared to the other three countries. HUS has a different structure of spell data from the other three surveys. First, HUS stores spell data in separate files, which contain all changes on for example labour market status over the period from the entry interview till the last wave in which the respondent is present. Secondly, these spell data are not consistently connected to a household identification number or connected to all separated household members. This makes it a bit complicated to find out what the labour market status is of a women who enters the panel and changes household status and labour market status several times.

The size of the survey differs across countries. GSOEP and BHPS have a bigger initial number of households than HUS and OSA. Since we analyse a specific group out of these households, namely women having a child during the observation period, we benefit from larger initial samples size and samples that focus on a young part of the population. HUS covers the population aged 18-74 whereas OSA covers the age groups 16-60. Regarding the representation of age groups in the population, we have more

Table 3.1: Observation Period, Frequency and Sample Size: GSOEP, BHPS, OSA and HUS

	GSOEP			BHPS	OSA	HUS
	Former WestG Germans	Former WestG Immigrants	Former EastG	Great Britain	Nether lands	Sweden
Start of data collection	1984	1984	1990	1991	1985	1984
Latest wave in this study	1992	1992	1992	1992	1996	1996
Year (s) for which retrospective information from data set is used	1983	1983		1980-90	1980-1985	
Frequency of data collection:						
Annual	x	x	x	x		-
Bi-annual					1985-86	1984-88, 1991-93
Tri-annual					After 1986	1988-91, 1993-96
Initial Number of households	4,600	1,400	2,200	4,600	2,000	2,300
Added in 1986						1,500
Added in 1993						500
Added in 1996						1,000
Selected ages	16+	16+	16+		16-60	18-74

Sample D of GSOEP not included since we do not use this sample in Chapters 4-7.

chance of observing women aged 18-45 in OSA than in HUS, all else equal. In addition the attrition rate, and whether additional samples have been collected determines the number of observations in our fertility and work sample. Furthermore national differences in fertility rates will also lead to different probabilities of finding birth events in the surveys.

Household Data collection

All four data sets are organised on the household level by household identification number as well as on the individual level by individual identification number. The household level is used to determine (changes in) household composition. The information on household composition is provided by the head of the household. Individuals provide information on changes in labour force status, their earnings etc.

Definition of the household Regarding multi-member households some of the surveys use refinements from the basic definition 'a group of people living on one address'. GSOEP applies this basic definition, whereas BHPS and HUS view a household as a group of people who either share living accommodation, or share one meal a day (BHPS) or one or more meals a week (HUS) and for whom the address is their only or main residence. Up to six months continuous residence during the year was a minimum requirement. The OSA survey imposes two additional criteria on the basic definition. First, only household members in the age group 16-60 (since 1990:16-64) who are not in the military service or in full-time education are considered as household members to be interviewed. Secondly, selected household members must all participate in the entry interview. If a household continuously participates in the survey, then the second criterion is not imposed any more.

Definition of the head of the household Surveys differ in appointing the head of a multi member household. GSOEP leaves the classification of the head of the household to household members themselves. BHPS uses as criteria for classification 'legally and financially responsible for the accommodation', or 'the eldest of two people equally responsible'. In the OSA survey the head of the household is the person who contributes the largest share in total household earned income. The HUS survey has the general rule that for married couples and couples living together in a marriage-like relationship, the man is designated as head of the household. An exception is made if the man is expected to be absent for longer than six months in the year of interview. For households in HUS with several adults, and for households with several married couples, the individual with the highest income indicated in the survey is determined to be household head.

Which household members are personally interviewed? All household members who passed the age of 16 are personally interviewed in GSOEP, BHPS and OSA.[28] The HUS survey on the other hand questions only household members older than 18. The maximum number of participating adult household members is three and the information on household members between 16 and 18 years old is provided by the household head in HUS. Information on children younger than 16 in GSOEP, BHPS and OSA is provided by the household head.

Data collection method The German, British and Dutch survey is collected mostly by personal and telephone interviews. The Swedish survey is collected differently across waves. In 1984 all HUS interviews were personal interviews. Since then the design has been to administer personal interviews to respondents at entry into the panel and subsequently interview these persons by phone. The HUS waves of 1988 and 1991 consisted only of self enumerated mail questionnaires, with a non response persons follow-up by phone.

Identification of persons and households during the panel period We need 'fertility and work' information on the selected women and their spouses over the observation period, or at least information from one wave before and one wave after the child is born. This means that the selected women, their spouses and the households of which they are part, have to be traced across the panel waves. A general rule is that the household head remains in that position in subsequent waves, irrespective of any changes in household composition. Therefore the relationship between household members and the head of the household is important. There is no difficulty if the woman and her spouse stay in the same household. However, if the woman or her spouse leaves a survey household, or joins a new survey household, or the woman and her spouse both decide to form a new household, and this is by design in each household panel survey a new survey household, then we need to be able to identify the woman and her spouse in the new household. The household panel surveys do not deal with

---

[28]   Surveys included in this study exclude persons who live in an institution or abroad.

this identification similarly. The GSOEP and HUS assign a second household number to a person who moves into a new household. This means that a person is identified by the established personal number assigned at entry, the household number assigned at entry and a new household number. A different procedure is used by the Dutch OSA and the British BHPS. These surveys assign a second person number to a person who moves into a new household, consisting of the number of the new household plus the person (rank) number within the household.

Attrition

In order for an observed birth to be included in the analyses of labour force transitions in connection with child birth, and the changes in the earning positions of a woman before and after childbearing, the recent mother has to be observed in two or three subsequent waves around the date of birth of the child. The analyses of the timing of maternity and the analysis of the timing of return to work after childbirth and the timing of having subsequent children requires of course that the woman is in the panel as long as possible and that all the information on labour market behaviour and earnings of herself and of her spouse is updated as long as possible. According to Wagner, Burkhauser and Behringer (1993) the attrition rate has been relatively low in the GSOEP. They mention that through eight panel waves, 54.9% of the original panel respondents have longitudinal records without missing years. New households which are often founded by the split-off of a young person from an old household have a higher probability of leaving the panel. Most of the observed births in the BHPS come from the retrospective calendar. Therefore there is no panel attrition. However, attrition plays a role for the 1991-1993 period, but it is not very high. Seventy nine per cent of the original BHPS sample members who participated in a complete interview at wave 1 also participated in wave 3. Praat (1996) mentions that only 22% of the original OSA sample in 1985 is still present in the 1994 wave. The HUS survey benefits from little panel attrition due to the efforts of the HUS data team to include persons who left the panel during the period 1984-1993 back in the panel of 1993 and persons who left in the period 1993-1996 back in 1996 ("Bortfallsundersökningen").

Birth events in a woman's life

We detect all first, second and third birth events during the panel period of each survey, using all available waves, the monthly retrospective information on fertility history, and separate spell data files on changes in household composition. Because labour market behaviour around first birth potentially differs from behaviour around subsequent births, birth order is an important distinction. Table 3.2 presents the number of women and their 'birth events' according to birth order.

Birth events are requested in the interview section on changes in household composition during the period between waves for the whole observation period for Germany and Sweden, for Britain for the period 1991-1992, and for The Netherlands for the period 1985-1996. The 'birth' event registration in all four data sets is in dates (year/month) in order to avoid the problem of "referring to the previous 12 months" in combination with "different interview dates during a field interview period that takes several months".

By using the request on the number and date of birth of all biological children, addressed to women at entry of the survey,[29] we find birth order of the new born in the household/ the woman's fertility record. In GSOEP, BHPS and OSA children have their personal ID number but in HUS children under the age of 18 are connected to adult household members and not registered by a personal ID number.

In GSOEP, the respondent's marital history and the fertility history for female respondents were specifically asked for at entry of the survey. During the GSOEP period the household questionnaire only consults year and month of birth of children present in the household. Each wave of GSOEP changes in household composition are requested in the personal questionnaire. In the case of a birth, the month of birth of the child is requested. This procedure is the same across all waves. Somewhat peculiar is, if there are three women in the household they all answer that a child is born in the household. However, it is not known or asked, who is the biological mother of the child. Cases were dropped where it was not possible to determine which child belonged to which woman in the household. This mainly occurred in the Immigrant sample in former West Germany, when several families lived in one household. Therefore GSOEP does not provide information on whether a child, born during the panel

---

[29]   For example:This request is in the OSA family form ("gezinsformulier").

Table 3.2:   Number of Women and Children Born During Observation Period

	WG	Imm.	EG	GB	NL	S 84-93	S 84-96
First child only	283	128	67	355	374	59	
Second child only	111	64	44	a	a	51	
Third child only	52	55	13	a	A	50	
First and second child	157	57	1	440	302	60	
Second & third child	34	16	-	a	a	19	
First, second & third child	28	1		172		8	
N of women	665	321	25	967	676	247	
N of 1st child	468	186	68	967	676	91	146
N of 2nd child	330	122	45	612	302	105	131
N of 3rd child	114	72	13	139		55	

Source: G=Germany GSOEP (1984-1992):WG=Former West Germany; Imm.= Immigrants in Former West-Germany;EG=Former East-Germany, GB=Great Britain BHPS (1991-1992, 1980-1990 retrospective), NL=The Netherlands OSA (1985-1996, 1980-1985 retrospective) and S=Sweden HUS (1984-1993/96). N=total number; a)= not applicable: for BHPS (1980-1990) and OSA we rely on retrospective data, which means that we do not observe only second or third births. Third births in the OSA survey not selected.

period is the biological child of the women. Births are found in the OSA similarly as in GSOEP, but the request on information includes whether the child is biological.

In HUS it is possible to distinguish between biological children and children who joined the household by adoption or as a child of a partner. If the woman gave birth to her first biological child and there is already a child in the household from a former marriage of her spouse, we analyse the birth as a first birth.

The requested household composition is not standard across waves in the HUS survey. All HUS waves contain information on the year and month of birth of biological children of the female respondent at the point when she enters the panel, except for the 1984 wave which does not request the month of birth of children. Fortunately, the lacking month of birth and whether the child is biological or adopted can be figured out of the spell data files on changes in household composition. However, the 1991 wave of the HUS lacks data on the number of children female respondents have given birth to and the year of childbirth according to birth order. Therefore, we compare the number of household members and the number of children (as household members) and their birth years in the waves 1988 and 1991 to see if there is an increase in the number of children present in the household.

These spell data in HUS are stored in separate files different from the other surveys. They contain all changes on household composition, both information on persons joining or leaving, an ID number of the household, or the ID of one or more household members. The attachment to a household ID, or ID's of household members is not standardised across spell files. The reasons why persons join the household are among others cohabitation, marriage, divorce and birth of a child. The number of persons that join or leave, and per person the month and year of leaving or entering is registered.

We use the fertility history data collected at a woman's entry of survey for the period 1980-1990 in Great Britain and for the period 1980-1985 in The Netherlands. These retrospective fertility data, include the date of birth in year and month of women's children.

Since we observe only part of a life course, some of the detected births are first, some are second and some are third births. Births of higher order than three are rather few and we decided not to analyse these. Therefore the cases in our analysis include women who are observed to have given birth to their first child, others who have given birth to their second child, others who have given birth to both first and second child and so on.

Labour market histories around births

We organised the data on labour market participation around the date of arrival of the child in the household to indicate women's labour market status at defined dates before and after having children and also to indicate the period of 'home caring time' after the birth of a child. Going through the calendar of labour market events we know the labour market status each month around the date of childbearing, when the woman enters the labour market after giving birth, and whether or not she reports any break at all. All four countries collect monthly information on the labour market status of household members during the observation period. The BHPS and the OSA provide this information retrospectively for the period 1980-1990 and 1980-1985 respectively. In her analysis of the quality of retrospective data, Dex 1991, concludes that a broad summary of employment history can be collected with a reasonable degree of accuracy. She cites Freedman et al.

(1988) who show that in 1985 83% of respondents confirmed their labour force status for a month of 1980.

Table 3.3 shows the categories in labour force status in the surveys. GSOEP, BHPS, OSA and HUS differ some what in the number and definition of the categories. For example, GSOEP and BHPS use different categories for full-time and part-time employment, whereas OSA leaves a person the possibility to indicate his/her own hours of work per week. HUS registers the changes in weekly worked hours more precisely, in spell files (on changes in weekly hours, categorised as in Table 3.3) separated from the spell files on changes in labour market status. As the different categories stating full-time (Voll-Erwerbstätig) and part-time (Teilzeit-beschäftigt oder geringfügig Erwerbstätig) work in GSOEP and BHPS are not defined in hours worked per week, we assume that persons have the official statistics in mind when providing the information. In official statistics a full-time working week means 35 hours/week or more. In OSA we categorise the hours of work per week, and in HUS we use the the official statistics.

Unfortunately OSA does not distinguish between (different categories of) leave and being employed.[30] Also the HUS does not make a distinction but includes all kinds of leave, vacation and so on into one variable. This makes it difficult to compare OSA and HUS information to the category 'maternity leave' in GSOEP and in BHPS.

---

[30]   On the other hand OSA gives very detailed information on other aspects. For each new situation a person experiences on the labour market, OSA reports on a monthly basis: weekly worked hours separated into normal time, paid and unpaid overtime. Further OSA reports whether the change in labour market status is voluntary, the reasons for the change in labour market status, among which are reasons associated with changes in household situation like marriage and birth; the net earnings after the change in labour market status; whether the change means a different profession or occupation or tasks (job-job mobility), and whether the change means a lower/same/higher status job. The later two sources of monthly information are also available in HUS spell files. The OSA surveys in 1994 and 1996 only report the change in labour force status without reporting any information on changes in weekly worked hours on monthly basis.

Table 3.3: Labour Force Status in Employment History Calendar and Spells

Germany	GSOEP	Great Britain	BHPS	The Netherlands OSA	Sweden	HUS
		Self employed		(andere) werkkring als zelfstandige "meewerkende echtgeno(o)t(e)" andere functie bij dezelfde werkgever		
Voll erwerbstätig		Full time paid employment		(andere) werkkring in loondienst	gainfully employed	
Teilzeitbeschäftigt oder geringfähigg erwerbstätig[a]		part time paid employment		respondent's own indication of hours pw	hours pw categories: <15 >=15 hrs<24 >=25 hrs <34 >=34 hrs <44 >=44	
Arbeitslos gemeldet		Unemployed		werkloos	Unemployed leave:vacation, etc	
Im Mutterschafts-/ Erziehungsurlaub		Maternity leave				
Hausfrau/Hausmann		family care			keeping house	
Auf der (Hoch)Schule		full time student		dagopleiding	Schooling	
In betrieblicher Aus-bildung/Fortbildung/ Umschulung						
		Long time sick, disabled Government training scheme				

Except for the categories in Table 3.3 also the categories 'retired','military service alternative service' and 'something else' are recorded., but not included here, since these cathegories are not relevant for our sample of women. a) these are small jobs, no tax and social premium contributions. In the total German sample of 1992 only 1.4% of the interviewed persons were in this type of job (Vlasblom 1998).

For Great Britain 1980-1990 and OSA 1980-1985 respondents automatically participate in the fertility history calendar and in the labour market history calendar. The retrospective monthly fertility and work calendars are found as part of each wave in the GSOEP and the OSA (1986-1996), covering a one and two year period respectively. HUS, on the other hand, merges all the spells on changes in labour market status from all waves into a separate file. This means that all labour market changes from 1984-1993 are found in one file for a woman who participated in the

1984 survey and who stayed in the panel till 1993. This file consists of an identification number, the labour market status, the starting date of the labour market status, the ending date, the duration and the order of the change in labour market status. There is a similarly constructed file that registers changes in the weekly worked hours on a monthly basis. Because vacation, sick leave and so on, are included as a separate labour market status, there are for example women in our fertility and work history files for whom we observe 20 different labour market spells. Using those 20 spells we have to find the spells around birth by searching in the labour force spell file for months preceding and after the date of birth to get a value on for example 12 months before birth categories from the spell file on hours of work per week.

In the analyses we lose 'birth' events when we require information about for example the labour market situation of the mother 12 months before she had the child. The same loss of observations occurs for women who gave birth to a child at the end of the observation period. The longer the period around birth taken into account, the more observations we will lose. There is monthly labour market calendar information available from 1.1.83 in GSOEP onwards. For the Swedish women who gave birth in the first three months of 1984, we do not observe the labour force status 3 months prior, and we do not know the labour force status 12 months prior on a monthly basis. Information is requested on employment in the calendar year predating the wave, but this is not on a monthly level. On the other hand, we know that if the woman indicates she was in employment during the whole previous year, she was employed also 12 months before the birth in 1984. However this information is less detailed. We do not know then whether she was on leave in the particular month around the birth we want to analyse.

In finding women's labour force status at certain points of time after having a child, the attrition rate and frequency of data collection within surveys are important. A higher attrition rate in a data set has as a consequence that we are less likely to find the labour market status 24 months after birth. High attrition combined with low frequency of collection will decrease the probability of finding the labour force status at a later date after the moment of having a child even further. The more frequent a survey is held, the more accurate the information on monthly changes on labour market status (including months of vacation or other leave) will be. However, there is a risk that persons will not participate in the survey anymore because it is held too frequently. The monthly information on labour market status is also collected for the "former drop-outs" sample in HUS. However, HUS does not provide monthly information on changes in weekly worked hours for this group.

Finding husbands and/or cohabiting men

We expect the human capital and earnings of the spouse to have an influence on women's decisions regarding participation in paid work in the period they plan to and actually have children. Therefore we need to add information on the spouse to the fertility and work files. To find out who the partner of the selected mother is during the childbearing period, we use the section on household composition for each wave of each survey, which is completed once per household by the household head. The relationship between household head and other household members is explicitly asked for in GSOEP, BHPS, and OSA. Slightly different, the request on household composition in HUS is filled out by a selected individual. However, this person is in most cases the head of household, and the relationship between selected individual, household head and other household members is explicitly asked for. On the other hand, although the HUS section on household composition is similar across waves, as far as new respondents/households are concerned, the 1991 wave lacks the corresponding information on the relationships between selected individual, head of the household and other household members. Therefore it is difficult in some cases in HUS 1991 to infer who is the spouse of a woman belonging to our fertility and work file. This occurs for example when two women and a man live in a household. It may be difficult to infer whether a first female household member is married/living together with a male second household member or whether the latter is a married male household member (e.g. her father) and she is a single daughter. Changes in household composition between waves are to be found in the spell data files on changes in household composition. If we have identified a man living with one of our sample women before birth we assume that the same person also lives with her after birth unless otherwise indicated in the data.

In the BHPS during the period 1980-1990 and in OSA survey during the period 1980-1985, retrospective information makes it is more complex to find out who was the spouse at the time of birth of the child. BHPS provides the marital history. If the woman was living with a spouse at the time of birth who is no longer her spouse in the survey sample of 1991, or 1992, there is no human capital and earnings information of the spouse she was living with at the time of birth. However, from the marital history variables we know the order of the marriage and how long they have formed a couple at time of birth of the child. OSA does not request the period the couple have lived together or were married. Therefore we do not know whether the spouse at survey date was also the spouse of the woman at time of birth of the child for the retrospective period. However, the retrospective period is short in OSA, namely 5 years as compared to 10 years in the BHPS. The shorter the retrospective period the less likely is a change of spouse particularly if there is a small child in the household, because divorces are considerably less likely among women with small children (Becker, Landes and Michael 1977, Chiswick and Lehrer, 1990).

Earnings of women and men around the date of having children

Information on pre-tax earnings of women having a child and their spouses is needed in all four analyses presented in Chapters 4-7. The analysis of the 'continuous career mother' determinants, and the models to explain women's timing of return to work after childbearing, women's timing and spacing of childbearing, all include pre-tax earnings of the spouse. The analysis of the optimal age at maternity and the analysis of women's earnings before and after childbearing include women's hourly wages before the birth of the first child. Therefore, additional information is needed on the hours in paid employment per week that corresponds with the monthly earnings.

The birth of a child is dated by year and month. Women's average earnings are requested from the interview week. Therefore, the period between the measurement of earnings before the birth of the child and the date of birth differ between women in our sample. Likewise the period from birth to survey week after birth will differ among individual women.

The analysis of women's earnings position before and after having a child is performed for former West Germany and Sweden. This analysis can not be carried out for Great Britain because information on earnings is only available for 1990-1992. The Netherlands is also not included in this analysis since gross earnings have only been requested in OSA waves of 1994 and 1996.[31] However, the optimal age of maternity in The Netherlands

---

[31]   In principle the analysis of women's contribution to family earnings around the birth of a first and a second child in The Netherlands can be conducted for the period 1992

[continued on next page]

can be analysed by using gross hourly wages in 1996, and net hourly wages during 1985-1996.

Since women's earnings might change substantially one or two years around the birth event, the definition of 'before birth' and 'after birth' has to be similar between the samples of West Germany and Sweden. Pre tax earnings is reasonably comparable between GSOEP and HUS. In Germany and in The Netherlands unlike in Sweden, vacation money is paid like an extra 13 month salary. However timing before and after earnings brings us the following difficulties. The difference in frequency of data collection (West Germany annually, Sweden, bi- or tri-annually see Table 3.1, complemented by information on 1989 and 1990 in the 1991 wave of HUS), means that if we solely use pre-tax earnings as similarly requested in GSOEP and HUS, the frequency of HUS data collection allows us to analyse births in 1985, 1987 and 1992. We then lose most of the birth events, namely those births that occurred in 1984,1986, 1988 till 1991, 1993 and 1996. However, two other sources of information on earnings which are available in HUS, make it possible to include more Swedish cases of women's earnings before and after having a child, than those with a 'birth' in 1985, 1987 and 1992.

Table 3.4 presents the question(s) posed on earnings in GSOEP, HUS and OSA. Employed Germans are asked their "Arbeitsverdienst brutto letzter Monat" including paid overtime work plus other benefits excluding vacation benefits. In the subsequent wave vacation benefits are included in a question concerning different categories of payment during the past year but there are many missing values due to panel attrition and non-response. Swedish HUS data provide three ways of measuring gross earnings. First, similar to the request in GSOEP, Swedes were asked to state their earnings before taxes according to the form being paid, hourly, weekly, monthly or yearly. Secondly, HUS requests employment income in the year prior to the interview, "inkomst av tjänst". Thirdly, HUS respondents have been asked whether they would allow a match of HUS survey information to tax register information on income earned. In the 1984 survey about two thirds of the respondents did allow such a matching.

---

to 1996. In surveys 1986-1992, like in the changes of labour force status, changes in net earnings due to changes in labour force status were asked for. We leave this to future research.

Table 3.4:   Information on Earnings in the Household Panel Data Sets

	The questions about income are worded in the following way:	Wave/year
GSOEP	Earnings before tax and social premium contributions Arbeitsverdienst brutto letzter Monat, includes paid overtime work plus other benefits excluding vacation benefits.	84-92
OSA	Can you tell me your earnings before taxes and social premiums? Do not include any extra's (van ploegendienst, overwerk, fooien, reiskosten-, representatie-, of vakantie-vergoeding etc.);the first amount on your pay check	94,96
HUS	How much do you normally earn before taxes per week, every two weeks, per month, per year, per hour. The information on average earnings in 1986 is "before taxes and other deductions". In 1984 the question is after deductions.	84, 86, 88, 89, 90, 91, 92, 93 not add., 96
	There are two questions on 'inkomst av tjanst':	
	1. 'How much did your income from employment amount to in the calendar year prior to the interview?'. This includes wages, insurance payments, pensions, but excludes capital income and deductions from employment. In 1988 and 1991 this includes deductions from employment. Prior to 1988 income from employment has been reduced by SEK 3,000 (schablon=travel cost compensation).	84, 86, 90, 91
	2. 'How much did your cash earnings amount to in the year prior to the survey year. This is usually the major part of 1.	84, 86, 93, (also add)

GSOEP: German household panel data set; OSA: Dutch household panel data set; HUS: Swedish household panel data set. BHPS, British household panel data set is not presented in this table since a request for earnings (gross and net) is available per wave, and we only have wave 1991-1992. Request for net earnings is left out for GSOEP and HUS, we use only gross earnings in the analyses of Germany and Sweden.

The tax register information is also available for all three data sets in 1993: the panel, the former 'drop-outs' of 1984-1993, and the additional sample of 1993. In 1993 74% of the panel respondents, and about 89% of the additional sample and the sample of former 'drop-outs' gave permission. For all three 1993 groups, when respondents gave permission, tax register information is available for 4 years: 1985, 1987, 1990 and 1992. The information from the tax registers is employment income, so it can be compared to the direct question. Information on earnings by tax register is not available in GSOEP.

Data on earnings is only available for the employed, excluding the self employed. Using the information on labour force status, persons with zero earnings, because of not being employed are included in our sample, rather than to lose these observations. The survey request that a person indicates whether (s)he was at work the week prior to the interview. HUS applies a slightly different definition of "employed" than GSOEP, which does not give specific information for those on leave or expecting to return to work soon. In HUS 'employed' means that the respondent performed paid work during the last week or that (s)he had time off, was ill or on leave for less than 8 weeks, or that (s)he expected to return to work within one week. Therefore Swedish persons for whom we do not have information on earnings could be either not employed or on leave for more than 8 weeks or not expecting to return within one week. "Looking for work" means that the respondent was looking for work or was laid off and did not expect to return to work within one week. "Not in the labour force" means that (s)he was either unemployed, retired, disabled, keeping house or was a student and was not looking for work, or (s)he had time off or was ill or on leave, and this had been the case for more than 8 weeks.

Pre tax hourly wages are to be found by dividing monthly pre tax earnings by hours worked per week times number of weeks per month. GSOEP and HUS[32] provide similar and consistent over time (across waves within the survey), information on hours worked per week. In GSOEP this is called "Tatsächliche Wochenarbeitszeit" which is weekly worked hours including paid and unpaid overtime work. We do not have information on average worked hours per week for those on leave for Germany. Like the information on earnings, the information on average hours of work per week is only available for employed people in HUS, which implies that we do not have information for those on leave for more than 8 weeks.

HUS provides two other sources of information on hours worked per week. First, weeks spent on various activities, including full time and part

---

[32] The question on 'hours of work per week' is worded as follows: "On average how many hours per week are you currently working at your main job, including paid and unpaid overtime?". In :1984, 86, 88, 91 93 (also for former drop outs).

time employment in the calendar year prior to the interview is requested.[33] Unfortunately this information is only available for 1983 and 1985. Secondly, there are spell-data on (changes in) hours worked per week, but this information is in categories (see Table 3.5), which does not make it possible to distinguish between working e.g. 25 and 33 hours. This information is not relevant for this study, because it is not comparable to the other Swedish or GSOEP requests on weekly hours of work.

We computed earnings and wages for countries into constant prices of 1993 in national currency.[34] All information in national currency is corrected for the difference in purchasing power by using the Purchasing Power Parity exchange rates.[35]

Comparing education across countries

Our comparative analyses between Germany, Great Britain, The Netherlands and Sweden require comparable definitions of a variable such as the highest completed level of schooling. However, this variable is differently reported in each survey, because of internationally different educational systems. We make the highest completed level of schooling comparable between countries by considering the years it generally takes to complete different levels of schooling.

Each survey requests personal characteristics like age, schooling level and employment experience since age 16 during a person's entry interview. First, the entry interviews of the women and their spouses included in the fertility and work file have to be detected. Then, we update the schooling and work experience information to the date of birth of the

---

[33]   The retrospective method starts with: 'How many weeks did you spend on leave?'. Several other categories then follow and the last questions concern the weeks spent on full-time and part-time employment. Finally the interviewed person is asked how many hours per week (s)he worked during the weeks stated as full-time work and how many hours during the weeks working part-time.

[34]   Correcting for changes in consumer prices shows that there are larger differences in prices over time in Sweden than in Germany, The Netherlands and the United Kingdom. For example: Earnings of 1984* (consumer price index93/consumer price index 84)= earnings 84 at 93 prices, means that earnings of 1984 are multiplied by 1.83 at 1993 prices for Sweden and German earnings of 1984 are multiplied by 1.23 at 1993 prices.

[35]   For 1993 (OECD, 1996): US$==1:Germany: 2.103 DM /US$, Great Britain(UK) 0.637 B£ /US$, The Netherlands 2.134 Dutch f/US$ and Sweden 9.833 SEK/US$.

child, using monthly information on additions, available in labour market spell files.

Internationally comparable educational levels for the countries in this study are presented in Table 3.5. The GSOEP requests the highest attained level of education. A person's attained educational level is requested by Allgemeinbildender Schulabschluss, Beruflicher Ausbildungsabschluss and Hochschulabschluss. These three categories are specified in subcategories. If more than one Abschluss (per category: Schule, Ausbildung, Hochschule) is attained, a person indicates the highest him/herself.

Using information on the number of years it generally takes to finish schooling (Schulabschluss), and specific types of vocational training (Bildungsabschluss) and the years it generally takes to finish Hochschule on top of the requested attainment before entering the Hochschule, four basic categories of schooling are constructed: 1: Hauptschulabschluss, anderer Abschluss, Kein Abschluss; 2: Realschulabschluss; 3: Fachschule; and 4: Abitur, and 5 categories which a person can have on top of these 4 basic categories. These categories on top of the basic categories of schooling can be Berufliche Bildungsabschluss and/or Hochschulabschluss. The first category is 'Beambtenausbildung' which takes 1,5 years. The second category is Lehre, Berufsfachschule, Schule, Gesundheitswesens, Sonstige Ausbildung which all take 2 years. The third category is Fachhochschule which takes 3 years. The fourth category is Fachschule which takes 4 years. Finally, Universität, TH/Hochschule im Ausland all take 5 years.

The GSOEP does not request years of schooling or years spent on vocational training comparable to BHPS, HUS or OSA. Information on years of schooling in GSOEP can be obtained from the biography activity calendar, providing the main activity each year from a person's 15th birth year till they participate in the survey.

The BHPS and the HUS request the highest completed level of schooling, and the years of vocational training (in full-time equivalent, in HUS this refers to training at a training institution including practical training as part of a study program), the last calendar year of full-time education and the total number of years spent in a full-time educational program. Furthermore the most recent year a person participated in vocational training is requested, including only full time training lasting more than one month or the equivalent. The British educational system differs between England and Wales on the one side and Scotland on the other side. In England and Wales, 16-19 year olds can obtain several

Table 3.5:   Comparable Educational Level out of Household Panel Data Registration

A	B	age at attained educ. level*	GSOEP Germany	BHPS Great Britain	OSA Netherlands	HUS Sweden
		Age at start	6	5	4	7
1	I	12-13		CSE Grade 2-5, Scot grade 4-5	lagere school	
		14-15	Hauptschul/ anderer Abschluss	Commercial qualification, no O-level		Folkskola
2		15-16	Realschul- Abschluss	GCE O-levels or equivalent	MAVO/VBO/ LLW	Grundskola
		16-17	Fachschule		HAVO	
3	II	17-19	Abitur	GCE A-levels	VWO	student examen
4	III	19-20		Nursing qualification	MBO	
		20-21		Other higher qualification, teaching		
5		21-22			HBO	
		22-24	Universität. T.Hochschule	First degree	universiteit	Universitet
		25		Higher degree		

The detailed information on the survey questions are described in appendix Table 3.1. *The assignment of 'years it generally takes to complete different levels of schooling' benefitted from the help of J.D. Vlasblom (GSOEP), A. A. McCullough (BHPS), and S.S. Gustafsson (HUS). McCullough also assisted in comparing the school system in England/Wales and Scotland. A:These 5 comparable levels of schooling we use in some of the analyses of Chapters 4-7: 1. Only compulsory school or less, 2. More than compulsory school but not high school, 3. High school: German: Abitur, British 'A-level', Dutch: HAVO/VWO, Swedish: Studentexamen, 4. Some college or vocational training on top of high school and 5. university graduate or more. B: In some analyses we work with three levels of education: 1. less than high school, 2. high school and 3. more than high school.

qualifications within a framework of General Certificate of Education (GCE), A-level qualification, broad based General National Vocational Qualification (GNVQ's), and job specific National Vocational Qualification (NVQ's). International comparability is obtained by assigning years of schooling to the level of schooling using OESO (1996).

The OSA survey is more detailed than the other three surveys in using an education history calendar to register exactly how many years a person spent in what type of schooling after the first compulsory eight years of education, whether this has lead to completion of an educational level, which one, and when this level has been completed. Also on the job training and reasons for changes in the labour market situation have been administered on a detailed level. In waves 1994 and 1996 a somewhat different approach was used by showing detailed charts with all different schools that could possibly be visited. The Dutch education system is derived from the 'columnized' society, so there are many parallel schools of different denomination covering the same age groups of students but with different profiles. The completion of different schools have been recoded to 5 educational levels according to the "Standaard Onderwijs Indeling, 1978" installed by Dutch Central Bureau of Statistics. Assignment of years of education to the level of education is according to the Dutch Department of Education, OCW (1997).

Comparing years of experience in paid work between countries

An important explanatory variable in the analyses of chapters 4-7 is the years of experience in paid work of women and their spouses at the time of birth of a child. This variable 'experience in paid work' indicates the ability of the woman and of her spouse to get a price for schooling and training. Information on the number of years of employment experience till the date of entering the panel is obtained in the first interview. The entry question on 'work experience since school leaving' differs in the surveys as regards full-time and part-time registration. The years spent in employment may include years in part-time work and/or months of full-time work but only part of the year. If the part-time category is not specified in hours per week or months per year, we recomputed 1 year part-time work, and full-time work during part of the year, as 0.5 year full-time work per year. After the first interview the information on a person's employment experience is updated by the monthly spell information on changes in labour force status, till the date of having a child. The spell data on labour force status differ in their precision of registration of full-time, part-time, categories of hours worked per week, as described in section 3.4 on labour force status. Table 3.6 shows the questions on employment experience in the surveys included. Information on experience in the labour market in OSA is available, except for 1988 and 1990. For those who enter the panel in waves 1988 and 1990, and stay in the panel, their total experience in paid work is found in a subsequent wave giving the total work experience till date of interview.

Table 3.6: Employment Experience (Years) at Time of Having Children in Household Panel Data Sets

	Survey questions on years of employment experience:
Germany (GSOEP)	Entry: What have you been doing since age of 15? (activity biography, annual, slightly different categories than Table 3.3) Spell: What have you been doing in the calendar year before the interview (Activity calendar spell, monthly, see Table 3.3)
Great Britain (BHPS)	Employment history calendar: from the date of leaving full-time schooling, all successive employment status in full-time and part-time.
The Netherlands (OSA)	1985: How many years have you been in paid work till the 1st of January 1980? Please do not count interruptions. After 1.1.1980 request for detailed information on labour market participation till interview date in 1985. New respondents during survey period have been requested to give total years in employment till date of interview, except for new respondents in 1988 and 1990.
Sweden (HUS)	Entry: What have you been doing since school leaving age? Specification how many years part time or part of the year? How many hours per week during those years, and how many months? Work as an unpaid assistant and vacation jobs included, but no work lasting less than one month. Spell: Labour force status (Sysselsättning) and weekly hours worked (Veckoarbetstid) monthly (see Table 3.3)

Over the two years prior to the interview monthly information on labour market behaviour is requested, which can be used to indicate the employment experience prior to the interview, in 1988 and 1990. The request at entry of the panel on total years of employment experience does not account for the difference in years spent in full time and part-time work. This makes the answers less reliable compared to the other surveys. Once work experience since leaving school is known this can be updated, similarly to the procedure in the other surveys (see section 3.5).

Since we work with retrospective information on births and labour market situation of the women giving births in the period 1980-1990, the years in employment for our selected women and their spouses is constructed out of the employment history calendar in BHPS. For the years 1990-1992 the experience in paid work persons had when they first enter the panel is updated in the same way as in the other three countries.

Conclusions

We selected women from the household panel data sets at precisely the same moment in their family building cycle, namely at the point of having a child. Monthly information on the labour market status of household members enables us first to analyse the labour market status of the women at an exact date before and after having a child. Secondly, this offers the possibility of analysing the time of re-entering the labour market after having a child. Thirdly, human capital variables are updated till the month of having a child. Although we included precisely the same information for men as for women, we have not fully explored data on fathers in this study.

Similarities in data collection and period of observation across the surveys of Germany (GSOEP), Great Britain (BHPS), The Netherlands (OSA) and Sweden (HUS), still leave puzzles when making variables on education level comparable between Germany, Great Britain, The Netherlands and Sweden. However, by carefully comparing levels of education, assigning years of education to levels assisted by 'natives', five comparable levels of education have been constructed. Differences in frequency of data collection and requested information over time within a survey required careful comparison of waves. If the initial sample size is small, attrition rate in a survey is high, requested information changes over time or all possible combinations of these causes the 'work and fertility' files become small. This is also the main reason why births of higher order than two and sometimes three are not included in the analyses of chapters 4-7.

4 Women's Labour Force Transitions in Connection with Childbirth

Introduction

It is well known that labour force participation of German and Dutch women is substantially lower than in Sweden. Particularly large is the difference between mothers of pre-school children in Germany and The Netherlands as compared to Sweden. In 1994, 55% of all German women participated in the labour force. The rate of labour force participation of German mothers with pre-school children was 46% (Statistisches Bundesambt 1994). In 1985, the labour force participation of all Dutch women was 42.5, whereas the labour force participation of Dutch women with pre-school children was only 26%. Labour force participation rates of Dutch women increased to 58.5 in 1996, and for women with pre-school children the increase was very large to 57% in 1996 (OSA, Kunnen et al. 1997). However, in 1997 the corresponding figures for Sweden were 75% among all women and 78% among mothers with pre-school children (Statistics Sweden 1998). In 1992 73% of British women worked in the market (OPCS 1993). Although the participation rate of British women had increased to a high level compared to the German and Dutch female participation rate, the %age of economically active women with children under 5 years had only risen to around 50%. This is far below the participation rate of Swedish mothers with pre-school children. Joshi and Hinde (1993) show that employment of British mothers with children under three years had increased from 18% in 1980 to 33% in 1988. Full-time work amongst British mothers has increased since the 1980s and the interval between leaving employment to become a mother and any subsequent return has become shorter (Dex 1984; Martin and Roberts 1984; Joshi and Hinde 1993; McRae 1991; Joshi et al. 1995).

The purpose of this chapter is to analyse labour force transitions around childbirth and the extent to which these lower labour force participation rates of mothers are explained by policies in connection with childbirth. Women will choose to remain working at home or to enter market work depending on the net benefits in a broad sense from choosing one of the alternatives. A number of factors influence this choice. These are, the tax and benefit system (Blundell 1993; B. Gustafsson and Klevmarken 1993; Zimmermann 1993), whether taxes are jointly or individually assessed (Gustafsson 1992; Gustafsson and Bruyn-Hundt 1991; Nelson 1991), day care subsidies, availability of good quality child care (Gustafsson and Stafford 1992; Leibowitz et al. 1992), the duration and replacement ratio of parental or maternity leaves (Sundström and Stafford 1992), the organisation of the school day and after school care, the availability of (part-time) jobs and finally regulation as regards leave for caring for sick children. In all these respects, Sweden has chosen a policy mix that benefits the two-earner family according to an ideology of individual responsibility and equal role sharing which began in the 1930s and 1940s inspired by the 1934 book by Alva and Gunnar Myrdal on the Population Crisis (Gustafsson 1994). Germany on the other hand, has chosen policies that benefit the one earner family according to the breadwinner ideology (Sainsbury (ed.) 1994; Gustafsson 1984, 1994; Gustafsson and Stafford 1994, 1995). The type of welfare state ideology also influences policy choice. Germany is the prototype of the conservative corporatist welfare state. Also The Netherlands till the 1990s to a large extent falls into this category. Sweden is the prototype of the institutional universal social democrat welfare state. A third type of welfare state is characterised as the liberal or residual welfare state with the United States as the prototype. Great Britain to a large extent falls into this category. In comparison to Germany, The Netherlands and Sweden very little government support to families with children exists and having children is seen as a private concern. Individual parents can enjoy better provisions than the national standards if they work with an employer who has as a result of negotiations conceded to better provisions. In Chapter 2 government policies on the family in former West Germany, The Netherlands, Sweden and the United Kingdom have been described in detail. On the breadwinner-individual model axis Sweden and Germany are on opposite sides: Swedish public policies offer facilities and subsidies to encourage the combination of work and family, while Germany is bread-winner oriented offering tax-benefits to one earner/one carer couples, long maternity leave period with low pay, part-time child care facilities and part-time school day. The Netherlands changed from mostly bread winner oriented social policies in the 1960s and 1970s to mostly equal role sharing social policies in the 1990s. On the breadwinner-individual model axis the United Kingdom takes a place in between the breadwinner and the individual model of governmental policies on the family.

The family policies in the former GDR in many respects resembled those of Sweden. There were in the period 1949-1965 a network of child care centres, kindergartens and facilities for free school lunches created (Zimmermann 1993, p. 215). Under pressure from low birth rates provisions were extended to enable East German women to combine work and family. Paid maternity leave with full net salary was extended to twenty weeks in the period 1972-1989 and in 1980 the proportions of children with a space in the child care centres was 61% (Zimmermann 1993, p. 216). However, reunification, which implies that institutions will change to West German standards, resulted in closing of the day care centres in former GDR, a dramatic increase in unemployment for both men and women, decreasing labour force participation rates for women and a drop in fertility from close to two children per woman to well below one child per woman. This placed East Germany considerably below the fertility rates in the former FRG, which are already low by international standards (Zimmermann 1993, (p. 238).

The outline of the chapter is as follows. The major part of the chapter is an empirical analysis. We use the household data sets of Germany (GSOEP), Great Britain (BHPS), Sweden (HUS) and The Netherlands (OSA), as described in Chapter 3. First, we analyse the labour market status of women before entering motherhood. Secondly we analyse the flows into and out of the labour force by considering the situation 3 months before birth and 24 months after birth. Women who were employed both 3 months before and 24 months after birth may have different, more career oriented characteristics than women who were home makers both 3 months before and 24 months after birth. Thirdly, we analyse the determinants of being a career mother. Next, we turn to the timing of entering market work and analyse the characteristics of early and late returners. Finally we offer some concluding comments.

Labour force participation before entering motherhood

Table 4.1 presents the labour force status of German, Dutch, Swedish and British women 12 months and 3 months before the birth of their first child.

Table 4.1: Labour Force Status of Women in Germany, The Netherlands, Sweden and Great Britain 12 and 3 Months before Birth of the First Child

Months	WestGermany Germans 12	3	Immigrants 12	3	EastGermany 12	3	Netherlands 12	3	Sweden 12	3	Great Britain 12	3
Paid-work							78.3	69.4				
Full-time work	75.6	67.7	48.2	40.0	83.0	66.1			56.9	51.1	73.7	47.3
Part time work long 25-34	6.3	5.2	6.1	2.7	2.1	12.9					5.1	4.0
short <25 hrs/w									18.1	9.1		
hrs/w									12.5	11.4		
In education	5.6	4.1	7.3	3.8	8.5	6.5			6.9	5.7	5.2	1.4
Leave of absence, sick, parental, vacation	-	-	-	-	-	-			4.2	14.8	1.1	9.1
Maternity leave	3.6	3.7	1.8	3.2	0.0	1.6			-	-		
Unemployed	3.6	7.7	4.9	7.6	6.4	12.9	3.8	2.5	1.4	2.3	5.0	5.8
Unpaid work at home	4.7	9.0	27.4	41.1	0.0	0.0	17.8	28.1	0.0	2.3	9.0	31.0
Other	0.6	2.6	4.3	1.6	0.0	0.0			0.0	3.4	0.5	1.4
N	447	465	164	185	47	62	500	595	72	88	946	943

Data: Germany GSOEP Germans and Immigrants in West Germany 1983-1992, East Germany 1990-1992; Sweden HUS 1984-1991; Great Britain BHPS 1992; The Netherlands OSA 1985-1996.

Twelve months before birth should indicate the situation before any adjustments in connection with birth has been made and three months could possibly be the beginning of adjustments.

Although the proportion participating in the labour market of first time mothers is highest in Sweden, the proportion of these being in full-time work is lower than in Germany and Great Britain. In this respect Sweden does not appear to be the work society it is usually considered to be and which is also the intention of the institutional welfare state.[36]

of the groups considered in Table 4.1 only immigrant women in West Germany are full-time home makers before they have children to any large extent: 27% 12 months before the first child is born and 41% 3 months before the first child is born. There is a considerable decrease in full-time work among all the groups of women between 12 months before having the first child to 3 months before having the first child. In West Germany part-time work does not increase during this period as it does in East Germany. Being on maternity leave does increase as the date of birth is approaching, and in Sweden this increase is relatively high. A rational Swedish mother to be should make sure her income is as large as possible right before birth. It is better to be on leave from a full-time job than from a part-time job. The drop in 'long part-time' and increase in 'on leave' between 3 and 12 months confirms such behaviour, but the low full-time participation rate does not. In East Germany the drop from 83% full-time a year before birth of the first child to 66% three months before birth is accompanied by an increase in total unemployment and an increase in part-time work. This may be a period phenomenon caused by reunification which resulted in an increase in unemployment in the new German states of former East Germany from 10% in 1991 to 21% in 1993. For women the figure is 28% (Zimmermann 1993). Similarly, the decrease of full-time and the increase of part-time work may be explained, if part-time work has been easier to find than full-time work. In West Germany the drop in full-time work is accommodated by increases in unemployment and unpaid work at home both

---

[36]   Esping-andersen (1990:28) states: "Perhaps the most salient characteristic of the social democratic regime is its fusion of welfare and work. It is at once genuinely committed to a full-employment guarantee, and entirely dependent on its attainment. On the one side, the right to work has equal status to the right of income protection. On the other side, the enormous costs of maintaining a solidaristic, universalistic, and decommodifying welfare system means that it must minimise social problems and maximise revenue income. This is obviously best done with most people working and the fewest possible living off of social transfers".

among German women and immigrant women. However, among German women both in West and East Germany, two thirds are in full-time work three months before the birth of the first child as against only 51.1% of the Swedish women. A rational East German woman before reunification, like the Swedish mother to be would maximise her earnings right before giving birth, but since reunification West German rules apply. Since German women do not lose maternity payment by going directly from school to motherhood we had expected that many more German women than Swedish women to have their first child right after finishing their education. This result may imply that German women make the most of their working life before becoming mothers because they know they will soon enter into the status of home maker; Ostner (1993) describes this as 'immobile waiting at home with a cooked meal for their family members living a patchwork and zigzag life'. In contrast, Swedish women know that they are expected to go back to work again.

The lowest employment rate 3 months before first birth is found among women in Great Britain (51%) and Immigrants in West Germany (43%). According to Table 4.1, the employment rate of British first-time mothers declines sharply between 12 and 3 months before birth from 79% to 51%. The most likely explanation is that during the observation period a high proportion of the economically active British women were not entitled to maternity leave. As McRae (1993) shows, they left their jobs when they were pregnant but not at a time particularly related to the statutory provisions. A large proportion of British women end up in leave of absence three months before birth but unlike mothers in Sweden and similar to immigrant women in Germany the largest proportion of British women end up in unpaid work at home three months before birth.

Because Swedish women lose benefits during parental leave if they have smaller earnings three months before birth, we had expected Swedish women to be more work-oriented right before birth than women of the other countries where benefits are unrelated to previous earnings. However this is not what we find. The tight labour market in Sweden until 1991 may have induced women into thinking that the risk of losing their job was small so that they chose to be on leave rather than to be at work. Physically demanding jobs also give pregnant employees the right to extended pregnancy leave.

Home makers and market career women

The purpose of this section is to examine the group of women with certain characteristics that are career-oriented in the sense that they were participating in the labour force until 3 months before birth of their child and returned to wage employment after the end of legal maternity leave. Ondrich et al. (1996) analysed the subsample of those returning after the termination of the protection period. By examining labour force status 3 months before birth and 24 months after birth we can construct four groups of women: those who were employed both before and after birth denoted (ee), those who were employed before birth but not after (eh), those who were not employed before birth but employed after birth (he) and those who were not employed either before birth or after birth (hh). Because the period after birth is 24 months and the period before birth, 3 months, we may expect a larger number of observations to be censored after birth than before birth, during the 10-year period 1983- 1992 for West Germany, the 8-year period for Sweden 1984- 1991 and the 3-year period for East Germany 1990- 1992 that we observe.[37] The choice of 24 months was to capture career-oriented women under the German provisions, which allow

---

[37]   The Swedish data show more observations 24 months after birth than 3 months before birth. One of the reasons is that we have two dates of beginning of the spell information for dating births and labor force transitions. The spell information starts on January 1st 1984 for births during the first 3 months we do not know labor force status three months before births. In 1986 1,000 individuals were added to the data set. For women belonging to the added sample spell information begins January 1, 1986 and we do not know labor force status three months before for children born in the first three months of 1986. The German data set has an identity number for children so one can start looking for births by the birth date of the children. The Swedish data set has identity numbers only for adults so one has to start with the women at the four survey dates 1984, 1986, 1988, and 1991, look at how many children they had at the survey dates and then find the actual birth dates in the spell data using information on changes in family composition. The total number of Swedish births identified in the period 1984-1991 were 105 first births, 111 second births and 67 third births. According to Statistics Sweden (1992) the proportion of first births among all births for the eight year period 1984-1991 averaged 41.8%, second births was 35.5% and third births 16.4%, and 6.3% were births of higher orders. This gives us a distribution among the first three birth orders of 44.6, 38.0 and 17.5 to compare to the births found in the HUS data which are distributed as 37.1, 39.2 and 23.7 respectively. We have an under representation of first births and an over representation of third births but we need not worry so much about it since the analysis to follow is birth order specific. The numbers in Table 4.1 indicate that Swedish women and immigrant women in Germany have more third births than any other of the women.

Table 4.2: **Labour Market Transitions of Women in Germany, Great Britain, Sweden and The Netherlands based on Labour Market Status 3 Months before and 24 Months after Birth according to Birth Order**

| | Employment rate | | | | Transitions (excluding censored observations) | | | | | |
| | before 3 months | | After 24 months | | | | | | | |
	lfp	n	lfp	N	ee	eh	he	hh	Total	n
West Germany 1983-1992, Germans										
First child	72.9	465	39.5	339	32.6	41.9	6.9	18.6	100.0	334
Second child	37.3	327	36.1	219	25.1	10.5	11.0	53.4	100.0	219
Third child	31.4	121	27.1	85	18.8	14.1	8.2	58.8	100.0	85
West Germany 1983-1992, Immigrants										
First child	42.7	185	35.1	111	24.8	16.5	11.0	47.7	100.0	109
Second child	32.6	132	28.6	91	20.0	11.1	7.8	61.1	100.0	90
Third child	31.9	72	33.3	51	26.0	8.0	6.0	60.0	100.0	50
East Germany 1990-1992										
First child	79.0	62	39.0	41	37.8	43.2	2.7	16.2	100.0	32
Second child	70.5	44	61.3	31	48.4	29.0	12.9	9.7	100.0	31
Third child	61.5	13	50.0	8	12.5	50.0	0.0	37.5	100.0	8
Great Britain 1980-1992										
First child	52.6	836	34.3	726	22.7	28.1	11.6	37.6	100.0	726
Second child	28.7	547	37.6	425	20.0	6.1	17.4	55.5	100.0	425
Third child	30.9	156	33.6	110	19.1	4.5	14.5	61.8	100.0	110

Sweden 1984-1991									
First child	71.6	88	57.8	83	46.7	29.3	12.0	12.0	100.0	75
Second child	57.3	103	73.0	100	49.9	7.0	25.7	17.4	100.0	87
Third child	74.1	54	70.6	51	51.0	24.5	18.4	6.1	100.0	49
The Netherlands 1985-1996									
First child	69.4	595	36.1	477	33.0	35.3	3.9	27.8	100.0	439
Second child	36.6	303	40.4	225	25.9	8.5	14.7	50.9	100.0	224

Data: Germany GSOEP Germans and Immigrants in West Germany 1983-1992, East-Germany 1990-1992; Sweden HUS 1984-1991; Great Britain: BHPS 1992; The Netherlands: OSA 1985-1996. lfp -labour force participation rate per cent, n=number of observations, e=employed, h=not employed at home, ee=employed 3 months before and 24 months after birth, eh, he and hh accordingly. Differences in the number of observations are caused by censoring in the spell data.

for 24 months job protection, whereas the Swedish job protection period is 18 months. For Great Britain, and The Netherlands this time span after childbirth may not be as useful at capturing career oriented women, because the job security period is only 6.7 months in Britain and 6 months per parent in The Netherlands since 1990 but only paid in public sector.

In each successive birth order among West German and Dutch women, the group of continuous labour force participants (ee) decreases while the group of continuous home makers (hh) increases to well over half of the women. Among Swedish women the group of continuous career women remains about half of all women who had their child during the observation period, also for the higher birth orders while the group of continuous home makers remains a minority of about 12% of all women having a child. The employment rate declines to 57.8 after the birth of the first child. The proportion of women in 'eh' is higher after the first birth, whereas the proportion 'he' is higher after the second birth. This is consistent with findings of Hoem (1993) and indicates that Swedish women are making use of the "speed premium", which means that maternity pay will be based on earnings before the first birth if the second child is born within 30 months after the first.

The labour force transitions in connection with child birth of East German women look much more like the Swedish ones than like the West German ones although these data are from after the reunification. This indicates that the infrastructure of East Germany has not yet totally changed into the breadwinner regime. The British low employment rates before and after birth are also reflected in the small proportion of 'ee' mothers in Great Britain. Only 23% of the British first-time mothers were employed three months before and 24 months after first birth. The findings of other British studies suggest that our proportion of 'ee' mothers is low (Macran et al. 1995) and that more mothers do return if we would have chosen an earlier month, for example 12 months instead of 24 months after childbearing. Because of the poorer maternity leave provisions, many British women return to work earlier. The short supply of day care and the costs of care will also contribute to some mothers either not returning to work after childbirth, or not continuing to work for much longer after they have returned. Also the transferable ZRA (see chapter 2) creates disincentives for secondary earners, mostly women to work. The proportion of recent mothers in Great Britain who are not employed 24 months after the second and third birth is much higher than in Sweden.

The next step in the analysis is to find out whether women with continuous careers and women who are continuous home makers have different or similar characteristics. Logit regressions were estimated on being an 'ee'-woman, and an 'hh'-woman. The probability of being an 'ee'-woman when considering women's own human capital and the income of her spouse is reported in Table 4.3. For German women in West Germany and for Dutch women the results tell a convincing story that the human capital accumulated by the women before the birth of the child matters in determining whether or not she is an 'ee' woman. The longer the education of the woman and the more labour market experience she had before birth the more likely she is to have a continuous labour force career. This is true irrespective of birth order. The breadwinner ideology would assume that wives of richer husbands do not have to work in the market so that we could expect a negative influence from husband's income on the probability of being an 'ee'-woman. Only for second births of West German women we see that the husband's income is significant. It then increases rather than decreases the likelihood of the mother being a continuous labour force participant. This suggests assortative mating in the marriage market rather than a breadwinner effect. For The Netherlands we do not find that husband's income is significant. Further we expected that women whose husbands relative to themselves had larger human capital would be less likely to be career women. In a more extended logit model we measured this by the difference in years of schooling but this variable was never significant, nor was the age differential significant. Finally it may be expected that women who do not intend to have another child may have a different labour force behaviour than women who expect to have another child in the near future. We entered a dummy variable for not having another child during observation period, but the variable was not significant. We performed logit regressions on being a 'hh'-woman (not shown) which mirrored the results of being an 'ee'-woman with opposite signs. The findings on the determinants of being an 'ee'-woman among immigrant women in Germany are similar to those for West German women; the woman's own human capital determines her behaviour while husband's income does not influence the woman's choice for a continuous career.

Joshi et al. (1995) study the 1946 and 1958 cohorts of British women. They suggest that polarisation has been occurring between low and highly educated women. Highly educated women who delayed their first birth, built up work experience before birth and were able to use the new

Table 4.3: Logit Regressions on the Determinants of Unbroken Labour Market Career (ee 3,24) of Mothers in Germany, Great Britain, The Netherlands and Sweden according to Birth Order (t-values in parentheses)

	W-Germans First	W-Germans 2nd	Immigrants First	Immigrants 2nd	E-Germans First	E-Germans 2nd	Great Britain First	Great Britain 2nd	Netherlands First	Netherlands 2nd	Sweden First	Sweden 2nd
Const.	-1.670	-2.541	-4.653	-7.167	-3.659	7.641	-5.554	-6.457	-7.058	10.698	2.034	0.294
	(-1.61)	(-1.67)	(-1.79)	(-2.61)	(-0.73)	(1.55)	(-5.12)	(-2.91)	(3.72)	(-3.81)	(0.78)	(0.13)
Agemo	-0.061	-0.131	-0.220	0.056	-0.344	-0.693	-0.107	-0.079	-0.087	-0.026	-0.131	0.119
	(-1.14)	(-1.76)	(-1.52)	(0.75)	(-1.02)	(-2.07)	(-0.91)	(-0.56)	(-1.25)	(-0.22)	(-2.04)	(1.49)
Smo	0.196	0.265	0.710	0.425	0.735	0.227	0.303	0.317	0.556	0.732	-0.030	-0.267
	(2.93)	(3.31)	(2.84)	(1.56)	(1.83)	(0.81)	(2.16)	(1.70)	(3.77)	(3.08)	(-0.16)	(-1.63)
Expmo	0.122	0.171	0.537	0.127	0.496	1.306	0.230	0.231	0.256	0.186	0.092	-0.055
	(2.55)	(2.68)	(3.48)	(1.69)	(1.58)	(2.35)	(1.98)	(1.64)	(3.95)	(1.73)	(0.68)	(-0.62)
Inc. Spouse	-0.144	0.247	-0.179	-0.126	0.244	0.107	0.187[a]	0.460[a]	-0.201	-0.320	0.072	-0.083
	(-1.60)	(2.20)	(-0.62)	(-0.40)	(0.43)	(0.22)	(1.28)	(1.80)	(-1.16)	(-1.06)	(1.35)	(-1.45)
N	266	188	93	73	30	28	645	383	216	136	61	73
Log L	-1581	-932	-298	-279	-159	-134	-2171	-1043	-1540	-652	-385	-464

Data: GSOEP 1983-1992; BHPS 1980-1992; OSA 1985-1992; BHPS 1984-1996; HUS 1984-1991. ee 3,24 = labour force participant 3 months before and 24 months after birth. Agemo, smo, expmo, Inc.Spouse = age of mother, years of schooling of mother, years of labour force experience of mother, spouse's income before taxes/1000 at the time of survey nearest before birth of child. (a) BHPS does not give information on income of the spouse. We used socio-economic status of spouse instead, which indicates whether the spouse is unemployed/inactive, or his occupation: unskilled, partly skilled, skilled manual, skilled non-manual, managerial and technical, professional. Third births are not included because we have too few observations maternity legislation and pay for child care. In their analysis, the age of the mother at child birth became insignificant when education and work experience were included since those who delay return are less educated and had their child at an early age.

The same findings can be seen in studies by Dale and Joshi (1992), Jenkins (1994), Gregg and Wadsworth (1995). Our results in Table 4.3 do not reflect similar polarisation, rather we find that the woman's own human capital i.e. education and labour force experience determine whether or not they were in market work both three months before and twenty four months after birth. We choose to specify the regressions in the same way for all countries although for Britain including the interaction between experience and age, and experience and education in the regressions did perform better, confirming the results of the above mentioned British studies.[38]

Turning to a similar analysis for Sweden we get much less precise and insignificant results. We are inclined to believe that these results reflect real differences, which can be explained by the breadwinner ideology versus the individual equal role sharing. Swedish mothers are able to combine work and family also with fairly small amounts of human capital. German and Dutch women can act according to the individual equal role sharing model only if they are well educated. If they are less educated the breadwinner ideology and institutions puts them into the home maker position.

The timing of entering the labour force after birth

In this section we analyse how long it takes before recent mothers enter market work for the first time after birth. We do not require that the woman

---

[38]   The logit regression for Great Britain including interaction terms was the following: eel = employed 3 months before first birth and 24 months after; agemol = age mother, ysmol = years of schooling mother; expmol = employment experience mother; eel = dependent variable (n = 645); t-values in parentheses.

-28.3   +0.938 agemol   +2.041 ysmol   -0.258 expmol-   0.076 agemol ysmol
(-3.65)   (3.12)   (3.82)   (-1.41)   (-3.41)
+0.050 expmol ysmol   -0.006agemol expmol
(3.06)   (- 1.59)

Experience has a significant positive effect when the first time British mother is highly educated. Older mothers are less influenced by their educational level than younger mothers; for them work experience is far more important.

remains in the labour market for an extended period.[39] Such a restriction on the data would lower the numbers because in all the groups studied there is a considerable amount of in and out movements. The figures in Table 4.4 are therefore not strictly comparable with the employment rate after birth 24 months as presented in Table 4.1. In Table 4.4 we present the cumulative proportion of recent mothers still not entering the labour market by three monthly intervals after birth controlling for the exposure to risk. Very few mothers were at work 3 months after child birth in any of the groups we studied. Leibowitz et al. (1992) find that as many as one third of US mothers are back to market work within 3 months after the birth of their first child.

Interestingly and consistent with the shorter job protection period, Dutch and British mothers entered a job considerably sooner after birth than women in Sweden and Germany. Already three months after the birth of the first child 28% of Dutch women returned to their job. It takes nine months before one quarter of British mothers are in market work after the first birth but after six months already 15% are employed. In this respect Great Britain resembles the United States more than it resembles Sweden and Germany. The differences between Sweden and Germany are very small when comparing the proportion of mothers who are employed when the child is 6 months old, and it does not differ between the first and second birth. When the child is twelve months old the Swedish mothers are much more likely to be in market work than the German mothers. This difference between the two countries becomes more pronounced as the child grows older. When the child is three years old 80% of Swedish mothers have entered the labour market compared to 55% of the German women and 43% of immigrant women in West Germany. (The East German figures suffer from the short panel.) When the child is three, the proportion of women observed in the labour market after birth is highest in Sweden at every birth order. But the Dutch Figure is almost on the same level as the Swedish figure with only 24% still full time at home.

In Table 4.5 we present proportional hazard models of the duration in months before entering market work for mothers after childbirth. The

---

[39] The proportion of entering the laborforce and staying in the same labor market status decreases with duration, e.g. after 24 months 81% of Swedish mothers have entered the labor market in our data, but only 56.6 fulfill the requirement of also remaining in the labor force for the nine consecutive months. Similar results are found for higher orders in the Swedish and German data.

Table 4.4: **Cumulative Proportion of Recent Mothers Not Entering the Labour Market by Months Since Birth and Birth Order: Germany, Sweden, The Netherlands and Great Britain**

Months since birth	First Birth						Second Birth					Third Birth				
	WG	Imm	EG	S	NI	GB	WG	Imm	EG	S	GB	WG	Imm	EG	S	GB
3	95	97	98	95	72	96	96	98	95	96	94	99	100	100	98	96
6	94	94	98	94	61	85	94	96	86	93	84	93	98	100	98	86
9	86	87	97	88	56	76	89	93	86	87	75	88	90	100	80	81
12	76	82	94	60	52	72	85	89	77	67	72	85	83	100	70	76
15	68	75	69	51	48	69	80	84	59	51	67	80	76	91	57	70
18	62	71	64	34	45	66	76	80	53	41	63	77	71	72	50	66
24	52	64	40	22	39	60	67	76	37	27	55	73	69	72	29	55
30	48	60	30	22	31	57	63	69	27	22	47	64	64	72	25	45
36	45	57	27	20	24	53	56	62	21	16	42	59	60	72	22	41
N	403	160	50	96	..	860	290	119	44	117	559	109	68	12	55	161

Data: Germany GSOEP; West Germany, Germans (WG) and Immigrants (Imm) 1983-1992, East-Germany (EG) 1990-1992.; Sweden (S) HUS 1984-1991, The Netherlands (NL): OSA 1985-1996; Great Britain (GB) 1980-1992 (retrospective data); (a) Maximum age of a British child is 12 years and maximum age of a Swedish child is 7 years. For West-German mothers the child can be 9 years and for East-German women the child can be two years old.

results of Table 4.5 tell a similar story as the selection into being an 'ee'-woman. We added a variable for the interaction of age and employment experience. This variable takes account of the fact that the same amount of employment experience might have different effects at different ages. Similarly at a given age different amounts of experience might have a different impact. Among West German women, at the mean experience, the older the woman is at the child's birth, the later she returns. At the mean age at childbirth, the more market related human capital she accumulated before the birth of her first child, the earlier she entered employment (see Appendix Table 4.6 for means). Income of the spouse has a significantly negative effect implying that women with richer husbands delay their entrance to the labour force. The job protection period in Germany has changed over time. Time dummies to capture those changes were never significant in contrast to the finding by Ondrich et al. (1996).[40] Also immigrant women in West Germany return quicker if they have more human capital. The only difference between immigrants and other West German women is that years of employment experience is the most important explanatory factor when analysing the tempo of entering the labour market after birth of immigrants, while educational level is most important for West Germans. This is irrespective of birth order.

The regression on the Swedish duration before entering work after second birth shows that education does not influence the timing of entering employment. After the second birth, a mother returns to work later the older she was at birth of her second child (at mean work experience). The positive interaction effect between age of the mother and her experience for second time mothers in Sweden indicates that at ages above the mean, more employment experience increases the tempo of entering the labour market

---

[40]   The regression with the time dummies for the first birth for Germany was the following: all variables measured at birth: agemo = age mother, smo = schooling mother, exmo = employment experience mother, incspse = income of spouse, sdif = difference in schooling between mother and spouse, agedif = difference in age between mother and spouse, last child = the first child = the last observed child.
-0.085 agemo   +0.129 smo   +0.063 exmo   -0.90 incspse   +0.016 sdif
(- 2.4)   (2.7)   (2.0)   (- 1.4)   (0.4)
-0.016 agedif   +0.347 last child +0.259 (after 1986&bfr 1988= 1)
(- 0.8)   (2.0)   (1.2)
+0.178 (after 1988&bfr 1990= 1)   -0.052 (after 1990= 1)
(0.8)   (-0.2)

Table 4.5: Proportional Hazards of Months before Entering the Labour Force after Childbirth according to Birth Order (t-values in parentheses)

	First birth			Second birth				Third birth		
	Germany West	Imm.	GB	Germany West	Imm.	SWE	GB	Germany West	Imm.	GB
Age mother	-0.061	-0.011	0.007	-0.116	0.021	-0.206	0.052	-0.153	-0.030	0.109
	(-1.60)	(-0.14)	(0.38)	(-1.96)	(0.49)	(-2.52)	(2.38)	(-1.29)	(-0.44)	(3.03)
Smo	0.117	0.128	1.043	0.188	0.206	-0.013	0.013	0.148	0.173	0.011
	(3.13)	(1.39)	(1.74)	(4.25)	(1.56)	(-0.22)	(0.43)	(1.78)	(0.65)	(0.24)
Expmo	0.211	0.864	0.090	0.053	0.489	-0.552	0.069	0.593	0.678	0.819
	(2.59)	(3.17)	(3.02)	(0.34)	(2.22)	(-2.02)	(1.41)	(1.45)	(2.67)	(0.82)
Age*Expmo	-0.004	-0.025	-0.002	0.0001	-0.014	0.018	-0.003	-0.013	-0.014	-0.005
	(-1.62)	(-2.32)	(-2.74)	(-0.23)	(-1.97)	(2.29)	(-1.75)	(-0.98)	(-2.03)	(-1.21)
Income spouse/1000	-0.118	-0.304	a	0.003	-0.130	0.009	a	-0.147	-0.161	a
	(-2.03)	(-2.16)		(0.05)	(-0.93)	(0.35)		(-0.96)	(-0.83)	
N	339	138	835	256	105	81	542	94	60	154

Data GSOEP 1983-1992: HUS 1984-1991;BHPS 1980-1992; East-Germans not included: we only have data for 1990-1992. This is too short a period to draw reliable conclusions. For explanation of variables see note to Table 4.4. [a] BHPS does not give information on income of the spouse, because it is retrospective data. We did not find a single significant coefficient for first and third children in the Swedish sample. Means and standard deviations corresponding to the variables in this table appear in Table 4.6.

after birth while the opposite is true at younger ages at second birth.[41] We do not find any significant results for first births, which may have to do with the fact that about 80% of Swedish women who have one child proceed to have a second child and it is profitable to have the second child soon after the first without reentering.

In contrast to the German and Swedish mothers, British mothers of 2 or 3 children are in employment sooner the older they are at childbirth. This result is consistent with other British studies which have found that career oriented women who are also highly educated, delay childbirth and return quicker after giving birth when their maternity leave has expired (Macran et al. 1995; Joshi et al. 1995). The variable that controls for interaction between age and experience turned out to be significant for the first child, revealing a positive effect of more work experience on return to work, but the effect declines with age at motherhood.

Conclusions

The purpose of this chapter has been to analyse and compare labour force behaviour of women around child birth in Germany, The Netherlands, Sweden and Great Britain. Whether women enter or reenter employment or not, depends on the benefits of market work against home work. There are differences between the three countries in this respect. We rely on social science research to uncover how broad political and social patterns differ between countries. These patterns place Sweden on the one hand and Germany and The Netherlands on the other hand on opposite extremes of the breadwinner versus equal role sharing scale with Great Britain in between. On another dimension, the market versus state solutions, comparing our three countries places Great Britain at one extreme, relying more on the market, and Sweden at the other extreme, sponsoring in-kind benefits and subsidies toward mothers and children. On this dimension Germany and The Netherlands lie in between. The patterns we find can largely be explained by these differences. For example, Swedish women can rely on a number of policies enabling them to combine work and family (see also Rönsen and Sundström 1996), and we also find that Swedish

---

[41]   This analysis does not account for whether the mother indeed has another child during our observation period. A mother who has her first two children 15 months apart will be both in the column for first and second child. In principle she could be entering employment 45 months after her first birth and 30 months after her second birth.

mothers are more likely than mothers in the other countries to have a job when their first child is 2 years old but not when the child is six months old. This is because Swedish mothers make use of paid parental leave. In Great Britain the maternity leave is much shorter consistent with the ideas of the liberal or residual welfare state to keep benefits down. In The Netherlands labour force participation rates of women were low for a long period and the bread winner orientation in social policy did not encourage women to combine a paid career and (young) children. One result of this is that more British and Dutch mothers have returned when their child is three months old and when their child is 6 months than in the other two countries.

The German tax and benefit system, kindergarten system and the organisation of the school day all assume a breadwinner model and thereby assume that women remain at home with their children. The picture that emerges from the analysis of this chapter is that those women who have large enough human capital do combine work and family even if their husbands' incomes are high.

We found that German women are more likely than Swedish women to work full-time until shortly before the birth of their child although the Swedish parental leave benefits are based on earnings before birth while the German 'Erziehungsgeld' is unrelated to earnings before birth. From the analysis we can conclude that East German women continue to enter employment after child birth in the period 1990-1992 although the reunification has meant that breadwinner arrangements of the former FRG are being imposed on them and child care centres are being closed. The behaviour of East German women bears more similarity to the behaviour of Swedish women than to that of West German women, which is another indication that institutions or the legacy of institutions matters.

We found that more Dutch and British mothers have returned when the child is six months old than Swedish or German women. But when the child is 3 years old, more Swedish and Dutch than British mothers have returned irrespective of child order. The proportion of West German mothers observed back at work when the second or third child is three, is far lower than the British proportion. For British, as for German and Dutch women, having accumulated human capital determines whether she is a career mother. But when analysing the timing of entering the labour market after giving birth, it turned out that unlike German and Swedish mothers, older British mothers return quicker than the younger mothers. Especially for the first child our results confirm the polarising effects found in other studies that career oriented women who are also highly educated delay childbirth and return quicker after giving birth when their maternity leave has expired.

Table 4.6:   Means and Standard Deviations (in brackets) Corresponding to Table 4.5

	First Birth			Second Birth				Third Birth		
	WestG	Imm.G	GB	WestG	Imm.G	Swede	GB	WestG	Imm.G	GB
Agemo	26.7	22.9	24.8	28.8	25.8	29.9	26.8	30.4	28.6	27.6
	(4.7)	(4.4)	(4.9)	(4.3)	(5.1)	(4.8)	(4.7)	(3.8)	(5.6)	
Smo	11.1	9.1	11.7	11.1	8.7	12.3	11.6	10.7	8.5	11.5
	(2.6)	(1.8)	(1.9)	(2.7)	(1.2)	(2.8)	(1.9)	(2.5)	(1.1)	(1.9)
Expmo	6.5	3.0	6.5	6.8	3.9	8.6	6.5	6.6	4.8	5.2
	(4.8)	(3.7)	(4.8)	(4.5)	(4.9)	(4.4)	(4.6)	(4.4)	(6.0)	(4.0)
Income spouse	3.4	2.7		3.8	2.8	8.8		3.9	2.8	
	(2.2)	(1.2)		(1.9)	(1.3)	(3.3)		(1.9)	(1.2)	
N	339	138	835	256	105	81	542	94	60	154

Income of spouse in national currency. in 1993 (OECD, 1996): 1 DM= 4.67 SEK= 0.30 £ = 1.01 D*f*. Agemo, smo, expmo = age of mother in years at childbearing, years of schooling of mother, years of labour force experience of mother at the time of survey nearest before birth of the child. Inc. Spouse is spouse's income before taxes at the time of survey nearest before child birth. a BHPS does not give information on income of the spouse on monthly basis, because it is retrospective data.

5 Women's Share in Earnings Before and After the Birth of Children

Introduction

In a seminal paper Sörensen and McLanahan (1987) analysed married women's economic dependency using public use samples from the decennial US censuses 1940-1980. They found that in 1940 the vast majority of married women were completely dependent on their spouses for economic support whereas in 1980 that complete dependence was true for a minority of women. However a majority of American women in 1980 still earned considerably less than their husbands and would have had to decrease their standards of living below the poverty line if they had to live off their own earnings. In 1940 among non-white US married couples, 9% earned equal or more than their husbands and in 1980 this was true for 24.4%. Among white American couples in 1940 5.6% earned equal or more than their husbands and in 1980 the corresponding figure had increased to 15.4%. Differences in labour supply between different groups of women accounted for the major differences. However not only women with young children in the US in 1980 had a high degree of economic dependence on their husbands but also older women who no longer had young children.

      Gustafsson and Bruyn-Hundt (1991) analyse data for Germany (1984), Sweden (1984) and The Netherlands (1988) and find that married women on average contribute a small fraction of joint family earnings. For Germany the earnings contributed by the wife is 15%, in Sweden 28.8% and for The Netherlands 11.9%. Taking account of income tax systems after tax in the three countries German women contribute 12.4%, Swedish women 31.1% and Dutch women 11.6%. The largest difference between the three countries is for women with young children. Mothers with children 0-2 years old contributed 7.2% in Germany, 24.6% in Sweden and 6.6% in The Netherlands based on before tax earnings. Gustafsson and

Stafford (1994) find that labour force participation and hours of work of mothers with young children differ very much between the three countries. For example are 44.5% of US mothers of 2-3 year olds are non-participants against 73.2% Dutch mothers and 23.9% Swedish mothers. The Netherlands in the 1990s experienced a very rapid increase in female labour force participation also among mothers with young children. Kunnen et al. (OSA,1997) found that 57% of mothers with young children were labour force participants in 1996. These observations taken together indicate that labour force transitions around childbirth may be a significant determinant for future labour force participation and earnings. Labour force transitions are the subject of analysis in Chapter 4. The main findings are that before birth of the first child, German, Dutch and British women are at least as likely to participate in paid employment as Swedish women but they are far less likely to be found in paid employment once they have become mothers than are Swedish mothers. By the time the first child is 24 months old the employment rate among German mothers is 39.5, compared to 36.1 among Dutch mothers, 34.3 among British mothers and 57.8 among Swedish mothers.

This chapter focuses on the analysis of earnings of mothers in Germany and Sweden, computing women's earned income as a proportion of family earnings before and after childbirth. We are interested in the economic vulnerability that women experience around childbirth. The outline of this chapter is the following. First we construct birth histories by using all waves of the household panel data sets to determine when a birth occurred. Then we use information on earnings for the women and their spouses, taking one survey before birth and two surveys after birth, which is approximately two years, to compute women's contribution to family earnings before and after giving birth. Next, we analyse the determinants of share of earnings of the wife decomposed into predicted wage, probability of labor force participation and predicted hours of work given labor force participation simplifying the analysis by assuming husbands income to be exogenous. We hypothesise that human capital accumulated before birth of first child will determine earnings during and after mothering of preschool children. We find evidence for this hypothesis. However we also find that across our two countries there are differences in labor force participation and hours of work for the same predicted wage. We interpret these differences as a result of different family policy regimes which make it more feasible to combine work and family in Sweden than in Germany.

Finally we carry out a simulation holding characteristics of Swedish mothers constant and applying the German regressions and vice versa.

Data and definition of variables

In this chapter we work with the German Socio Economic Panel (GSOEP, 1983-1992, native Germans) and Swedish Household Market and Nonmarket Activities Panel (HUS, 1984-1996). We use our constructed fertility history and work file (See chapter 3). In this chapter we analyse first and second births only and disregard births of higher parity. The reason for this disregard is that there are very few births of parity three and higher in our data sets. On the other hand the distinction between births of different birth order is important since labour force participation and earnings of the mother are likely to differ very much for example comparing behaviour before first and before second birth or comparing behaviour between births to behaviour after last birth. Unfortunately we cannot know if an observed birth is the last birth because this type of panel data produces by its nature right censored observations. We choose to analyse all first births and all second births, which means that our constructed samples of first time mothers and second time mothers are two different samples. In some cases they overlap since some women have both their first and second child during our observation period. We would not confine our sample to this subset because we work with small samples.

The surveys contain information on human capital variables, earnings and hours worked of the mother and her spouse. From the German data we use the sample on native Germans in former West Germany. Both the German and the Swedish samples are restricted to those cases where we have information on earnings of the mother and her spouse (including both married and cohabiting men, from now indicated as spouse or husband) both before and after birth.[42] We define the wife's contribution to market earned household income as the proportion of the wife's earnings of the sum of the wife's and the husband's market earnings.

Ideally we would like to observe the mothers at a given point in time before and after birth of the child. We know month and year of birth and labour force status of the mother on a monthly basis but earnings, hours of

---

[42]   The data sets do not give information on who the father of the child is. In most cases the husband of the mother is also the father of the child but exceptions may occur.

work per week and other explanatory variables of the mother and of her spouse have to be taken from the surveys. The GSOEP in every annual survey provides monthly labour force status information between surveys while HUS provides the monthly information in separate spell files. Respondents have recorded their activity on a monthly basis according to about 8 different kinds of status including gainfully employed, full time unpaid work at home, unemployed, full time student, retired or on leave (see also chapter 3). In GSOEP maternity leave becomes a separate category in labour force status from 1988. Before this survey the maternity leave category is recorded when women choose "other" as they're labour force status and matched some other criteria. Maternity leave in HUS is included in a leave category that also contains sick leave and vacation. In GSOEP there are two categories for 'gainfully employed', full time gainfully employed and part time gainfully employed. In HUS information on full time and part time employment can be obtained from the spell files on monthly changes in weekly hours worked according to 5 different groups of hours worked.[43]

Because we want to compute wage per hour for our analysis of earnings capacity we need hours worked per week and earnings of the mother and of her spouse around the date of birth. The HUS surveys are less frequent than the GSOEP. HUS surveys were carried out in 1984, 1986, 1988, 1991, 1993 and 1996 whereas the GSOEP has been carried out annually from 1984 onwards. Interviewed persons in HUS were asked to state their earnings before taxes according to whether they were paid by the hour, week, month or year. The HUS questionnaire asked people to state their normal hours of work per week including overtime which may be partly unpaid. The consecutive Swedish surveys are identical in this respect.[44]

Ideally we would like to fix the before mothering earnings at a date say 3 months before birth. However neither GSOEP nor HUS provides such information. We know month and year of birth and labour force status of the mother on a monthly basis, but earnings, hours of work per week and other explanatory variables of the mother and her spouse have to be taken

[43]   The hours classification is 1-15, 15-25, 25-35, 35-45 and 45+.
[44]   The question on weekly hours of work in HUS is worded: On average, how many hours per week are you currently working at your main job, including paid and unpaid overtime? The question on average earnings is worded: How much do you normally earn before taxes per hour, per week, every two weeks, per month, per year?

from the waves (see chapter 3). We choose to observe earnings and hours of work one wave before the wave in which the child is born and two waves after. When data on earnings in HUS were not available from a survey at most one year before birth, we used a variable on 'income from employment last year', in connection with hours of work for that year. The question on hours was then calculated on the basis of information on the number of months per year the person worked on a full-time basis, a long or a short part-time basis.[45]

The Swedish and the German data are comparable in survey information on average weekly hours worked. For Germany we used "Tatsaechliche Wochenarbeitszeit" which is weekly hours worked including paid and unpaid overtime work. Before tax earnings in the GSOEP are "Arbeitsverdienst brutto letzter Monat" which includes paid overtime work plus other benefits but not vacation money. The following survey year vacation money is included in a question concerning different categories of payment but there are many missing values on this question. This means that German earnings are understated in comparison to Swedish earnings because there is the habit in Germany to pay a 13th month of vacation salary which is not included in 'Arbeitsverdienst brutto letzter Monat' while there is no extra vacation money in Sweden. Swedes have to save from their twelve monthly earnings for their vacation. There may also be cases of German women who are on maternity leave and do not answer this question about last year or fill in that their earnings are zero. The Swedish wage variable is constructed from hourly wages or monthly earnings depending on the actual pay from the individual whereas the GSOEP always supplies monthly earnings information at the survey date. We calculated hourly wages by dividing monthly earnings by hours worked, whereas earnings were given on a monthly basis. We recomputed earnings and wages for both countries into constant prices of 1993.[46]

---

[45] There were two questions on earnings of the year before the survey in HUS: The first concerned 'Income from employment last year'. How much did your employment income amount to in 19(AA)? AA=survey year minus 1. Income from employment means total employment income, no capital income, but after deductions from employment. In 1988 and in 1991 the earnings are before deductions and have been reduced by SEK 3000 (schablon=travel cost compensation). The second question concerned 'Cash earnings in last year'. How much did your cash earnings amount to in 19AA.

[46] This means for example that earnings of 1984 are multiplied by 1.83 for Sweden and German earnings of 1984 are multiplied by 1.23 at 93 prices.

Swedish crowns have been translated into German marks by the purchasing power parity of 1993, which is one DM equals 4.71 SEK in 1993 (OECD 1995).

We use information on human capital accumulated by the mother at the time of birth of the child (see chapter 3). We believe that the best comparability across countries is achieved by working with 5 levels of schooling: 1. only compulsory school or less, 2 more than compulsory school but not high school, 3: high school: Abitur, Studentexamen, 4: some college or vocational training on top of high school and 5: university graduate or higher.

Women's contribution to family income

Whereas the long run effects of labour force interruptions on earnings have been researched both using cross sectional data (Mincer and Polacheck 1974, Corcoran & Duncan 1978, Dankmeyer 1996, Gustafsson 1981, Albrecht et.al. 1997) and using longitudinal data (Mincer and ofek 1982) this chapter focuses on the short run effects. We believe that the short run effects around childbearing are a major determinant of the long run effects on women's economic vulnerability.

The time of measuring earnings and work hours before and after childbearing, depends on whether the child was born right before a survey or after a survey. The earnings data are comparable across countries and before and after birth and across observations which are taken from all the different birth events from the early 1980s up to and including the early 1990s by the purchasing power transformation. Results are presented in Table 5.1.

We have identified 259 first births and 193 second births in Germany for which we have also been able to find earnings data for the woman and her husband both one survey before birth and two surveys after births. For Sweden we have identified 146 first births and 131 second births for which earnings information is available for the woman and her husband. In principle the earnings information is taken one survey before birth and two surveys after birth but as indicated above it is more complicated in the Swedish data because the surveys have not been annual and for some observations earnings information has been taken from the tax register information of 'earnings last year' which was merged to the HUS survey after permission had been received from the interview persons.

Table 5.1: **Monthly Earnings of Women and their Spouses One Year before and Two Years after the Birth of the First and the Second Child in Former West Germany and Sweden**

Panel A: All women having a first or a second child with family earnings>0

	N	Women's earnings		Spouses' earnings		Women's contribution to family earnings	
		Before	After	Before	After	Before	After
Germany							
First child	259	1,454	657	3,497	3,965	0.29	0.14
Second child	193	523	870	3,791	3,764	0.12	0.19
Sweden							
First child	146	2,124	2,014	2,753	3,069	0.44	0.40
Second child	131	1,993	1,699	2,973	3,247	0.41	0.34

Panel B: if women's hours in paid work >0 before birth of the child

	N	Women's earnings		Spouses' earnings		Women's contribution to family earnings	
		Before	After	Before	After	Before	After
Germany							
First child	154	2,286	845	3,469	4,039	0.38	0.17
Second child	58	1,659	2,303	3,877	3,020	0.30	0.43
Sweden							
First child	79	2,449	1,953	3,307	3,344	0.43	0.37
Second child	58	2,019	1,809	2,947	3,306	0.41	0.35

Panel C: if women's hours in paid work >0 two years after birth

	N	Women's earnings		Spouses' earnings		Women's contribution to family earnings	
		Before	After	Before	After	Before	After
Germany							
First child	91	1,762	1,976	3,266	3,736	0.35	0.35
Second child	46	1,746	2,060	4,087	2,547	0.29	0.45
Sweden							
First child	96	2,177	1,962	3,025	3,265	0.42	0.38
Second child	82	2,023	1,815	3,057	3,253	0.36	0.36

The major impression from Table 5.1 is that Swedish women go through the childbearing process without any substantial drop in earnings. The variation in the proportion of family income earned by the women in Sweden is from 44% before first birth to 34% after second birth. The smallest earnings of German women occur after the birth of the first child and before the second child when German women only secure 12 to 14% of family earned income. All entries in Table 5.1 show that German women have smaller earnings in comparison to their husbands than Swedish women have. Whereas Swedish women always lower their earnings after birth in comparison to before childbearing. This is true also for German first time mothers but not for German second time mothers who rather increase their earnings after their second birth in comparison to before their second birth.

In panels B and C we present two different subsets of the data given in panel A. Panel B is delimited to women for whom we know that their hours of paid work were positive before the birth of the child and panel C is delimited to women for whom we know that they had positive hours of paid work after the birth of their child. For both the German and the Swedish mothers this is substantially fewer women than the totals of panel A.

Restricting the German sample to those who worked for pay before or after birth of the child increases average earnings of the woman substantially whereas average earnings and wife's contribution hardly change for the Swedish women and the small change is even not in the expected direction. This suggests that Swedish women may have earnings although we do not observe them to have positive hours of work. The paid parental leave benefit may explain for this. During our observation period the paid parental leave benefit in Sweden was 90% of previous earnings for 12 months and a per diem for three additional months (see Chapter 2).

One of the reasons we have more observations on earnings than on hours of work is that we have occasionally used the tax register information. There is no retrospective information on hours of work data corresponding to this. The German data with annual waves and annual information on earnings and on hours of work gives more information and we also observe that average earnings change in the expected way. German women who worked two years after the second birth seem to be a select group. The results indicate that husbands of these women decrease their earnings after the second birth and that the average earnings of the women exceed that of their husbands. This indicates that these fathers may have decreased their hours of work maybe in order to make time free for care of the young child. Swedish husbands on the other hand in all three panels increase their earnings after birth of their child in comparison to before the child was born. In fact, in all three panels, German fathers decreased their incomes after the birth of the second child but increased their earnings after the first child.

Carlin and Flood (1997) show by using time use data and survey data from the HUS 1984 panel, that Swedish fathers do adjust their actual hours of work downwards when they have young children. Table 5.1 shows that men do not adjust their earnings downwards but rather increase their earnings from before they have a child to after the birth. However the variation in earnings before the birth of the child compared to after the birth of the child is only from one% to 12%. This result is of course perfectly in line with the Carlin and Flood (1997) result because most of the adjustment of working hours of Swedish fathers is done within the limits that the parental benefits system allows. The German data show much more dramatic changes both for mothers and fathers. Fathers increase their earnings after birth of first child and decrease earnings after birth of the second child. For the German mothers it is the other way around, namely, dramatic decreases in income after first child and substantial increases after the second child is born. The exception is in panel C where first time mothers also increase their earnings from before to after birth of the first child. In the next sections we will analyse to what extent the changes in income are due to changes in wages, labour force participation or hours of work for workers.

An explanation of the change in earnings around childbirth

Romantic love stories in the 1950s ended with a kiss confirming the decision to marry with the implicit assumption that the couple then lived happily ever after. The troubles of combining work and family were not in a young woman's perception. A young person of the 1990s is probably much more aware of this problem. Having a child is an important and joyful event in a young couple's life but very time consuming and for the woman it can also be very costly. The young man can count on being able to pursue his career interests and can also claim that this is in the interest of the family but for the young woman it is much more difficult. She may have to forsake her career and earnings for being a mother or she may have to forsake the joy of becoming a mother because her career demands do not allow mothering.

   This difficult 'either or' situation induces women to postpone the birth of their first child maybe sometimes to the point where there is no choice anymore. We therefore observe as low fertility rates as 1.2 in Spain and Italy where the combination of work and children has been regarded as a non-existent problem until recently. One scholar regards Italy as 'undertertiairized' (Bettio, 1996) i.e. having far too little supply of services, that might help the combination of work and family. The tertiairization can be market organised or organised by services supplied by the public sector for day care for children and elderly people. Many other aspects of the organisation of the society such as a match between school hours and office hours, increased shop opening hours, and access to banking and postal services electronically will facilitate the combination of work and family. However the basic fact that children cost time cannot be altered simply because children need their parents time and parents need their children. The joy of children that parents feel cannot exist unless time is spent together with the child. Realistically the younger the child the more time consuming. In fact Gustafsson and Kjulin (1994), using information from the Swedish HUS survey, show that time costs of children are larger for smaller children 1-3 years old than for children 4-7 years old. Both active child care time and time spent on total household work by parents were larger for the youngest children than for the somewhat older children.

   We want to decompose earnings of the mother after giving birth to a child. Our model can be written in the following way:

$$(1) \ y_t^a = p_t^a w_t^a (h_t^a | p_t = 1)$$

y_t^a in equation (1) is earnings of the mother after birth t, index t=1,2 for first and second birth, p_t^a is labour force participation of the mother after birth, which equals 1 if the mother participates in the labour force, otherwise it is zero, h_t^a is hours of work per week for workers. We then estimate the following set of equations:

$$(2) \ w_t^b = w_t^b (Hc_t)$$

$$(5) \ h_t = h_t(w_t^b, y_t^m) | \ p_t = 1$$

$$(2) \ w_t^b = w_t^b (Hc_t)$$

$$(4) \ p_t = p_t(w_t^b, y_t^m)$$

Wage before first birth w_t^b in equation (2) depends on the woman's human capital (HC) before birth for first and second births t=1,2. This regression is shown in Table 5.2 for German and Swedish women having a first birth. Wage after childbearing w_t in (3) depends on wage before childbearing for first and second births. Labour force participation after birth p_t in (4) depends on wage before birth and husband's income at the point of decision i.e. after birth. Weekly hours of work for labour force participants h_t (5) depends on wage before first birth and husband's income at the point of decision i.e. after birth. We are employing an individual model taking husband's income as exogenous for the woman.

Results of estimations on labour supply of recent mothers

Most studies of women's labour supply include variables on family composition, number of children and children's age (Killingsworth & Heckman (1986), Gustafsson (1992), Vlasblom (1998)). In this study we have instead selected the women at precisely the same moment in their family building cycle namely at the point of having their first birth or second birth respectively. The first step in our analysis includes standard human capital wage regressions (Mincer, 1974) on wage before birth. The reason for using wage before first birth as a prediction also for the second birth is because wages earned during the interbirth period may be of a more incidental character. The results are given in Table 5.2. For the German women we use the 154 women who have a positive wage observed before the birth of their first child (panel B of Table 5.1) to predict wage before first birth for all the 259 women who are observed to have a first child (panel A of Table 5.1). Similarly we use the 79 Swedish first time mothers who have an observed positive wage before their first birth to predict wage before first birth for all the 146 mothers who had a first birth during our observation period. The wage regressions of Table 5.2 perform reasonably well. Years of experience and the square of years of experience given education have the expected signs showing an increasing wage at a decreasing growth rate which is in line with human capital theory. The German set of dummy variables for schooling show the expected increase in wage the longer the education. The Swedish set of schooling variables are less decisive. For example, university graduates do earn less than women with some college or vocational training, but the t-values are not large enough to

Table 5.2:   Wage Regressions One Survey Before Birth for Recent Mothers in Germany and Sweden

	Germany		Sweden	
	Wage bfr 1stb	Means (st.d.)	wage bfr 1stb	Means (st.d.)
	OLS	2.580	OLS	2.638
	ln(w)	(0.44)	ln(w)	(0.48)
const.	1.794		1.664	
	(15.99)		(4.60)	
Schooling				
1=university	0.753		0.698	
	(4.31)		(1.96)	
2=	0.537		0.820	
	(3.78)		(1.78)	
3=	0.355		0.475	
	(2.56)		(1.09)	
4=	0.234		0.324	
	(2.37)		(1.90)	
5= <8 years				
5=base				
Expmo	0.105	7.56	0.082	6.37
	(4.98)	(4.29)	(2.81)	(4.9)
Expsq	-0.004	75.45	-0.003	64.2
	(-3.78)	(91.7)	(-2.60)	(104.7)
R2	0.31		0.26	
N (regression)	154		79	
pred.dep.var.	2.510		2.643	
mean (st.d.)	(0.31)		(0.21)	
n (prediction)	259		146	

Source: own computations based on all waves GSOEP (1984-1992) and HUS(1984-1996). Earnings and hours are found in the surveys, that is for Germany (GSOEP:1984,1985,..,1992), for Sweden (HUS 1984,1986,1988,1991,1993,1996). Mean age of the mother at first birth (observed wage) is 27.5 for Germany, 28.9 for Sweden.

conclude that there are indeed wage differentials between the different educational groups.

In Table 5.3 results of estimations of relations (3), (4) and (5) are given. We have based the number of observations for which we had information on all the relevant variables. For the regression on wage after giving birth to the first child there are 91 German women who are observed to have positive earnings two surveys after giving birth. However, we use hourly wage in the regression of Table 5.3 which requires information on hours worked. This is the reason we lose 6 observations between panel C of Table 5.1 and the wage regression in the first column in Table 5.3. The second column of Table 5.3 on labour force participation is estimated on 224 observations. For this regression we have made use of the monthly recording of labour force status which allows assessing exactly how many months it took before a recent mother entered the labour force after childbearing (see chapter 3 and 4). The wage and income variables perform with expected results for the labour force participation decision 24 months after birth of the first child for first time German mothers. The higher her own predicted wage is the more likely she is to participate in the labour force and the higher her husband's income the less likely she is to participate in the labour force. Between column 1 and column 3 we lose another 8 observations because of missing values on husband's earnings 24 months after the first child is born. However the regression of columns (4) through (6) shows a clear result that German second time mothers base their decision on hours of work and labour force participation on their predicted wage before first birth. The wage effect is positive implying that women with higher wages work longer hours i.e. the substitution effect is larger than the income effect, which agrees with other research on women's labour supply. Similar reasons as for first time mothers make us lose 1 observation in the regression of column (4) in comparison to panel C of Table 5.1 and 3 observations in column (6) in comparison to panel C in Table 5.1.

    Turning to the regressions of Swedish mothers columns (7)-(9) we observe that there is no loss of observations in column (7) to (9) in comparison to panel C of Table 5.1. However labour force status from the monthly spell data of the HUS on the basis of which we created the variable labour force status 24 months after birth of the first child was available for 113 women out of the 146 women who had a first birth during our observation period. Because the way the Swedish HUS data set has been collected and organised it has been a major detective work to search through all different files for the relevant information. The results of the Swedish regressions are less conclusive than the results of the German regressions. We find that the higher the first time mother's wage, the more likely she is to participate in the labour force but she does not base the decision on hours of work on her wage. Husband's income does not have a

Table 5.3: Wage, Labour Force Participation and Hours Regressions the Second Year after giving Birth for Recent Mothers in Germany and Sweden

	W-Germany						Sweden					
	After First Birth			After Second Birth			After First Birth			After Second Birth		
	(1)	(2)	(3)	(4)	(5)	(6)	(7)	(8)	(9)	(10)	(11)	(12)
	OLS ln(w)	logit lfp	OLShrs if>0	OLS ln(w)	logit lfp	OLShrs if>0	OLS ln (w)	logit lfp	OLShrs if>0	OLS ln(w)	logit lfp	OLShrs if>0
Const.	2.400	-0.836	19.886	2.263	-2.520	17.897	0.955	-0.377	20.851	2.364	1.534	19.43
	(22.64)	(-1.78)	(4.35)	(19.71)	(-4.56)	(4.40)	(2.90)	(0.04)	(3.71)	(11.3)	(1.14)	(3.48)
Pred.wage before 1st birth(a)	0.033	0.067	0.707	0.042	0.091	0.708	0.665	0.124	0.380	0.191	-0.049	-.0048
	(4.73)	(2.12)	(2.63)	(6.24)	(2.93)	(3.14)	(5.39)	(3.16)	(1.53)	(2.49)	(-1.17)	(-0.29)
Inc.spse 2 survs after 1st birth		-0.172	-1.817					0.194	0.849			
		(-1.92)	(-2.16)					(0.64)	(0.92)			
Inc.spse 2 survs after 2nd birth					0.147	-1.472					0.327	2.337
					(1.67)	(-2.29)					(0.86)	(1.57)
R2	0.21		0.12	0.48		0.23	0.24		0.11	0.15		0.12
Log L		-143.84			-102.88			-25.4			-22.6	
N (regression)	85	224	77	45	176	42	96	113	96	78	98	81
Pred.dep.var	2.93	0.37	22.92	2.83	0.32	20.45	2.77	0.83	30.02	2.82	0.84	26.5
(st.d)	(0.17)	(0.08)	(3.88)	(0.24)	(0.13)	(4.64)	(0.21)	(0.33)	(2.89)	(0.37)	(0.40)	(3.1)
N (prediction)	259	259	259	193	193	193	146	146	146	131	131	131

Data: GSOEP (1984-1992) and HUS (1984-1996). The variable labor force participation is from monthly information on labor force status and defined for exactly 24 months after birth. The variables wage, hours of work and income of the spouse after childbirth are taken from two surveys after the birth.(a)Table 5.2

significant effect on either a first time mother's labour supply decision or on a second time Swedish mother's labour force decision. This result is in line with results in Chapter 4 which showed that about 80% of Swedish mothers are labour force participants within 24 months after giving birth to a child.

Decomposition of after birth's earnings: a comparison between Germany and Sweden using simulations

In panel A of Table 5.4 we present observed means of the component parts of women's contribution to family income two surveys after the survey in which the child is born. In panel B of Table 5.4 we use values predicted from the regressions of Table 5.3 from own country regressions. The purpose of panel B is to show how well our simplified model can predict mother's contribution to couples' earnings using the regressions of Table 5.3. In panel C of Table 5.4 we analyse what the predicted values would be if the labour supply behaviour of recent mothers had followed the regressions estimated for the other country.

In Table 5.3 above there are three estimated equations for each country G, S (Germany and Sweden) and for each parity (t) 1,2 (first and second child birth) of the following forms:

(6) $\ln w_t = \alpha_0 + \alpha_1 w_t^b + \varepsilon_t$

(7) $\text{logit } p_t = \beta_0 + \beta_1 w_t^b + \beta_2 y_t^m + u_t$

(8) $h_t = \gamma_0 + \gamma_1 w_t^b + \gamma_2 y_t^m + e_t$

In panel B of Table 5.4 we predict women's hourly wage, women's labour force participation and women's working week using own country regressions according to :

(6') pred.own = $\ln \hat{w}_t^{\,G} = \alpha_0^{\,G} + \alpha_1^{\,G} w_t^{\,bG}$

(7') pred.own = $\text{logit } p_t^{\,G} = \beta_0^{\,G} + \beta_1^{\,G} w_t^{\,bG} + \beta_2^{\,G} y_t^{\,mG}$

(8') pred.own = $\hat{h}_t^{\,G} = \gamma_0^{\,G} + \gamma_1^{\,G} w_t^{\,bG} + \gamma_2^{\,G} y_t^{\,mG}$

and similarly for Sweden with superindex G changed for a superindex S. The mean of the individual predictions are given in Table 5.4. For labour force participation the probability derived from the logit regression is presented. In panel C of Table 5.4 we use the regression of the other country to predict women's hourly wage, women's labour force participation rate and women's working week. For Germany this is:

(6'') pred.own = $\ln \hat{w}_t^{\,G} = \alpha_0^{\,S} + \alpha_1^{\,S} w_t^{\,bG}$

(7'') pred.own = $\text{logit } p_t^{\,G} = \beta_0^{\,S} + \beta_1^{\,S} w_t^{\,bG} + \beta_2^{\,S} y_t^{\,mG}$

(8'') pred.own = $\hat{h}_t^{\,G} = \gamma_0^{\,S} + \gamma_1^{\,S} w_t^{\,bG} + \gamma_2^{\,S} y_t^{\,mG}$

For the Swedish predictions in panel C of Table 5.4 we used the German regressions (6), (7) and (8) and predicted wages, probability of labour force participation and hours of work given that the person participates in the labour force. The means of the individual predictions are presented in Table 5.4. In panel A of Table 5.4 we find that wages of German mothers who were labour force participants 24 months after birth are larger than wages of Swedish mothers but hours of work are smaller for German than for Swedish mothers so that the total difference in average monthly income of working mothers is within 200 Deutsche Marks per months i.e. 10% of a monthly income, see the third row of panel A of Table 5.4. The third row of Table 5.4A does not coincide perfectly with the numbers given in Table 5.1C because in Table 5.4 we have computed wages and hours of work and multiplied them, whereas in Table 5.1 we have used monthly income as reported in the respective surveys. Income of the spouse is taken as reported and coincides with the numbers given in Table 5.1. The proportion of wife's earnings in couples joint earnings for the subgroup of women who worked when their child was two years old, does not differ very much between Germany and Sweden. The variation is from 0.35 to 0.43 in row 4 of Table 5.4A. The large difference between Germany and Sweden is in labour force participation of mothers when the child is about two years old. Whereas 38% of first time mothers and 31% of second time German mothers were in paid work when their child was two years old, this was true for 77% of first time Swedish mothers and 81% of second time Swedish mothers. The average income of all German mothers including nonparticipants in the labour force is therefore less than half of that of Swedish first time mothers and less than one third of that of second time Swedish mothers. The resulting proportion of couple's earnings contributed by the wife is therefore not more than 16% for German first time mothers compared to 35% for Swedish first time mothers, and 12% for German second time mothers compared to 34% for Swedish second time mothers.

Table 5.4:   Mother's Contribution to Family Earnings 24 Months after Birth in Sweden and Germany Predicted Using own Country Regressions and other Country Regressions

	Germany 1st birth birth	2nd	Sweden 1st birth birth	2nd
A. Observed means				
1. wagemo/hrsmo>0	18.86	19.28	16.14	16.12
2. hrsmo/hrsmo>0	24.96	22.78	31.81	29.34
3. inc.mo=(1)*(2)*4.3	2,024	1,889	2,207	2,034
4. inc.spouse/hrsmo>0	3,736	2,547	3,265	3,253
5. contrib.w=(3)/((3)+(4))	0.35	0.43	0.40	0.38
6. lfp	0.38	0.31	0.77	0.81
7. inc.all=(3)*(6)	749	514	1,699	1,648
8. inc. Spouse all	3,965	3,764	3,069	3,247
9. contrib.all=(7)/((7)+(8))	0.16	0.12	0.35	0.34
B. Predicted by own country regressions and own characteristics[a)]				
1. pred.wagemo/hrsmo>0	18.72	16.94	15.96	16.78
2. pred.hrsmo/hrsmo>0	22.92	20.45	32.76	26.50
3. pred.inc.mo=(1)*(2)*4.3	1,845	1,490	2,238	1,912
4. inc.spouse/hrsmo>0 (obs.)	3,736	2,547	3,265	3,253
5. contrib.w=(3)/((3)+(4))	0.33	0.37	0.41	0.37
6. pred.lfp	0.37	0.32	0.83	0.84
7. pred.inc.all=(3)*(6)	614	481	1,858	1,606
8. inc.spouse all (observed)	3.965	3,764	3,069	3,247
9.pred.contrib.all=(7)/((7)+(8))	0.13	0.11	0.38	0.33
C. Predicted by other country regressions [a)]				
1. pred.wagemo/hrsmo>0	15.32	16.86	19.46	21.63
2. pred.hrsmo/hrsmo>0	32.17	29.25	25.00	25.17
3. pred.inc.mo=(1)*(2)*4.3	2,119	2,121	2,091	2,341
4. inc.spouse/hrsmo>0 (obs.)	3,736	2,547	3,265	3,253
5. contrib.w =(3)/((3)+(4))	0.36	0.45	0.39	0.42
6. pred.lfp	0.82	0.83	0.39	0.29
7. pred.inc.all=(3)*(6)	1,738	1,760	815	679
8. inc.spouse all (observed)	3,965	3,764	3,069	3,247
9. pred.contrib.all=(7)/((7)+(8))	0.30	0.32	0.21	0.17

Source: own computations based on all waves of GSOEP (1984-1992) and HUS (1984-1996). See for definition of variables Table 5.3. [a)] Predictions are based on regressions from Table 5.3.obs.=observed

In panel B we analyse how well our simple model predicts the woman's contribution to family earnings. We come fairly close, within a few percentage points, with the biggest relative discrepancy being that the prediction for German first time mothers show that they contribute 13% of earnings in panel 5.4B whereas it is 16% in panel 5.4A and 14% in Table 5.1A. However the differences between our two countries are much bigger. Comparing panel 5.4C (pred.other) to panel 5.4B (pred.own.) shows that the Swedish regressions for given characteristics imply smaller wages, longer hours of work for labour force participating mothers and a larger labour force participation than the German regressions. The overall result is that German mothers would, given their characteristics, have increased their earnings from about 11 to 16% of family earnings to 30 to 32% of family earnings if they had behaved according to Swedish regressions. Furthermore, Swedish mothers would have decreased their earnings' share in the family earnings from about 33 to 38% to about 17 to 21%.

We believe that these differences can be ascribed to the fact that there are many more facilities to combine work and family in Sweden than in Germany due to better provisions in family policies such as paid parental leaves, subsidised full day care for children, the right for full-time workers to shorten work hours to a six hours work day until the child is 8 years old, long shop opening hours etc. The Swedish political history during most of the 20th century has been that of social democratic governments whereas the Federal Republic of Germany during most of its history has been dominated by Christian democratic governments with its stronger emphasis on traditional family values and mother's place in the home. For further discussion on family policies see Chapter 2 above.

Concluding remarks

This chapter is a contribution to the research on the effect of childbearing on women's career and earnings. Different from most research along these lines we study a more short term effect of a childbirth on earnings rather than the long run effect, which has been studied previously (Mincer and Polacheck 1974, Gustafsson, 1981, Mertens, 1998). We believe that the most vulnerable period in a woman's career and her future capability of providing for herself is the immediate period around childbearing. The degree to which earning and mothering can be made compatible is crucial for these effects. By using all available waves from the German (1984-1992) and Swedish (1984-1996) panel data we were able to construct birth histories and date earnings of mothers and fathers before and after childbirth. We show that German women earned a smaller proportion of family earnings also before they had their first child than Swedish women, but that this proportion becomes smaller after giving birth to the first child going from 0.29 to 0.14. Whereas for Swedish women the proportion of family earnings went from 0.44 before giving birth to the first child to 0.40 after they became first time mothers. The difference between the two countries was caused both by smaller labour force participation and shorter hours of work for labour force participants for German mothers in comparison to Swedish mothers for similar hourly wages and human capital characteristics before mothering. We interpret this as a result of differences in family policies between the two countries.

In this chapter we showed how German women lost substantial earnings during their childbearing period earning on average only about one third when their child was two years old of what they earned before they became mothers. Swedish mothers on the other hand earned 80 to 90% of their prematernity earnings when their child was two years old, both for first and second time mothers.

In this chapter we regarded husband's income as exogenously given. However the data also reveal that some German fathers adjust their incomes downwards after the arrival of a second child. Swedish fathers on the other hand do on average increase earnings about 10% after the first and after the second child, which would be normal for a three year period for a young male without adjusting work hours. This is a topic which we have not addressed in this chapter but it does suggest that the incompatibility of work and family in a minority of German cases is solved by the parents in a non traditional way, whereas the Swedish young parents solve their compatibility problem by having the mother work a six hours work day and the father remain in full time work.

6 Paid Careers and the Timing and Spacing of Births in Germany, Great Britain and Sweden

Introduction

This chapter examines panel data from Germany (GSOEP, 1984-1993), Great Britain (BHPS, 1990-1992, from 1980 retrospective) and Sweden (HUS, 1984-1993) to analyse the timing and spacing of births in a woman's life.

Microeconomic theory of the family leads us to expect that women with a high degree of human capital (education and/or training) will delay the birth of their first child. However, in cases where the spouse is expected to earn a higher lifetime income, women are more likely to become mothers at an earlier stage. If we turn our analysis to the timing of subsequent births in connection with timing of work after first birth, microeconomic theory is less conclusive on women's behaviour. Women who are highly economically productive could opt for either a quick return to the labour market or to have a second child fairly soon, since both options would tend to minimise loss of human capital investment and returns from such investment. Economically less productive women would be in less of a hurry.

Differing government policies on the family, such as paid parental leave, the length of the job guarantee period, availability and costs of day-care provision for children, and family-related tax and fiscal benefits policy, may explain departures from microeconomic predictions in the three countries surveyed.

The outline of this chapter is the following. In section 2 we present economic theory on the timing and spacing of births. In section 3 we analyse how the predictions from economic theory are modified by public policies in the three countries surveyed. Subsequently, section 4 deals with the organisation of the data sets for the purposes of this analysis. Section 5 comprises the empirical analysis on the timing of first child and section 6 the empirical analysis of the choice between returning to work or having a second child. Section 7 concludes the analysis.

Theoretical considerations on timing and spacing of births

The purpose of this section is to analyse what economic theory can contribute to the understanding of timing and spacing of births, given that some women want to pursue a paid career in addition to raising a family. Following Cigno (1991) we can represent the financing of children as a lifetime budget constraint as follows:

$$(1) \quad \sum_{t=M}^{D} (C_t + B_t) r^{m-t} \leq y + \sum_{t=M}^{D} L_t w_t r^{m-t}$$

The lifetime budget constraint says that expenditures on adult consumption C_t and on children B_t over the relevant life span from marriage age M until the point of time D, (where the financial well-being of the children is no longer the parents' concern, here for simplicity's sake taken as the time of death) must be financed out of the lifetime incomes of the couple over the same period, discounted by the market rate of interest r-1. The husband's discounted lifetime earnings plus capital income are collapsed into a constant y in order to concentrate on the labour force behaviour of the wife. The child variable B_t has to be understood as the total expenditure on children in year t. The woman's market wage at time t is w_t and depends on her stock of human capital at that point in time. Time spent in market work of the wife L_t at time point t can be thought of as a zero one variable: either the wife is a participant in the labour market or she is not. In principle, however, the variable could also have any value between zero and one to indicate part-time labour market participation. We can then write the discounted present value of the lifetime cost of having a child at a particular point in time, t, as:

$$(2) \quad P_t = E_t + w_t + \beta \sum_{\tau=t+1}^{D} w_\tau L_\tau r^{t-\tau}$$

so that there is a component of direct expenditure E_t including clothing, housing, education and other monetary costs for the child in addition to time or opportunity costs. If we assume that the mother leaves the labour market during the time of having a child, the time costs of the child consist of the wage forgone in that period w_t plus the capital loss of human capital investment not undertaken during the child-caring period. In (2) human capital is assumed to increase linearly with the time spent in market work L_t as seen by β. The w_t or direct wage loss during the time spent full time at home for caring for the new born will be larger the longer the period of human capital investment prior to the birth and the capital cost which equals the third term of expression (2) will be smaller the fewer periods are left until time D.

In Figure 6.1 we illustrate some possible cases. Figure 6.1A shows the birth timing problem of a woman with a large potential growth in human capital i.e. a large β. If she has a child at time t_1 and returns to work at the end of that period, her direct earnings loss will be area A and her human capital investment loss will be the area delimited by the points abcd. On the other hand, if she waits until time t_2, her wage will have increased to w_2 and the direct wage loss will be area B and her human capital loss will be the area delimited by efcd. A comparison of Figure 6.1B to Figure 6.1A shows that if β is small, the human capital loss will be relatively unimportant. Numerous analyses of earnings functions have been carried out according to the Mincer (1974) specification:

$$(3)\ln w = \beta_0 + \beta_1 S + \beta_2 \exp + \beta_3 (\exp)^2$$

where the logarithm of the wage (ln w) is determined by years of schooling (S) and years of experience (exp) and the square of years of experience $(\exp)^2$. The results indicate that the square term is negative and statistically significant, which means that real life earnings functions are more likely to be of the character shown in Figure 6.1C than linear as in Figures 6.1A and 6.1B. If the age earnings function is non-linear as in Figure 6.1C, the human capital loss of an early birth might be considerable; whereas for late births it might be small as indicated by Figure 6.1C. In addition to the considerations of Figure 6.1 there may be human capital depreciation during periods of home time because knowledge may become obsolete or a person may forget job skills during absence from work. In such cases earnings w_t at return to work would be smaller at point b than at point a in Figures 6.1A, 6.1B and 6.1C. (see Mincer and Polacheck 1974, Gustafsson, 1981).

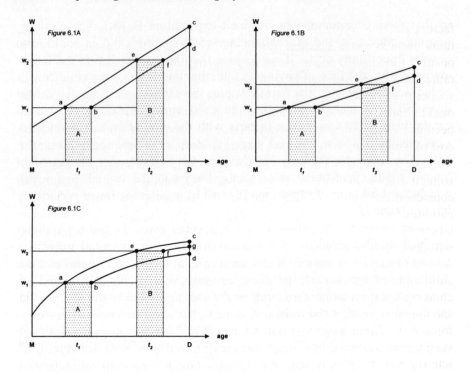

Figure 6.1: Theoretical Considerations on Timing of Birth

Hypotheses derived from theoretical considerations

Which hypotheses on the timing and spacing of births can be concluded from these human capital considerations? First of all, women who consider paid work and childcare to be incompatible i.e. those women who believe that a mother must be 24 hours present with her child should delay having children as long as possible since the loss of earnings and investment from the beginning of time period t_1 to time D is greater than the loss of earnings and investment from the beginning of period t_2 to time D. The postponement of motherhood should be longer the larger β, i.e. the more steeply the wage increases with labour market experience, since the corresponding areas in Figure 6.1B are considerably smaller than in 6.1A. The postponement incentive is strengthened if the age earnings function is non-linear as in Figure 6.1C.

It seems clear, then, that incompatibility of paid work with motherhood tends to favour later motherhood. However there are some factors pushing in the opposite direction in favour of earlier births. If we think of decisions as taken at time point M then the usual assumptions of a positive time preference could make couples prefer to have children sooner rather than later, other things being equal. The larger y in relation to (1) the sooner the couples are likely to have children.[47] Additionally, the larger the market rate of interest (r) the more unimportant earnings later in life become. This decreases the significance of the capital component in the cost of a child and makes timing less dependent on the human capital of the woman, so that there are fewer incentives to postpone childbearing. For women who plan to return to work and pursue their job career similar considerations apply, although for this decision problem the two parts of earnings forgone have to be compared in size. Also the shorter the intended labour force interruption the less important will the timing decision be. We will develop this reasoning in Chapter 7 below.

Let us now consider the situation of a woman who already has one child and desires a second, but wants to optimise the timing of the second child with respect to the total costs of the child (P_t) of formula (2). Should she immediately proceed to have a second child, making one longer labour force interruption, or should she first return to the labour market in order to keep up her human capital investment and then make a second labour force interruption for her second child? The trade-off between one period out of work in which clustered childbearing takes place against separate periods out of work for each birth will depend on whether the combined total length of the periods out of work can be the same, or whether there is greater risk of human capital depreciation when staying out for a single long period than when staying out of the labour market for two short periods. If the earnings function is linear as in Figure 6.1A, the choice between one longer labour market interruption for two births and two shorter absences for each birth gives equivalent results on earnings forgone and human capital investments forgone at a zero rate of interest. Further, just as is the case for the timing of a first birth, time preference and a positive rate of interest will speak in favour of clustering, i.e. one labour market interruption with a short interval between successive births. The non-linear nature of the earnings function as in Figure 6.1C, on the other hand, makes postponement of the second birth and labour force interruption more attractive. If there are major differences in the gradients of the age earnings

---

[47] One suggestion by Willis (1973) is to measure 'y' by predicted earnings at age 40 of the husband.

functions having a birth later will result in a much smaller loss of human capital investment forgone, which has to be compared to the direct wage loss during the period spent at fulltime child care. Also less economically productive women with a shallow gradient (β) have little to lose from poor timing of birth and labour market participation while other more economically productive women who have a steep slope (high value on β) have more to lose. Therefore we may expect differences in behaviour between these two groups. On the basis of these considerations we will form the hypothesis that more economically productive women with a high β will either return to work within a year or two or have a second child during this time period, whereas less economically productive women could operate at a slower pace.

Effects of family policies on timing and spacing of children in Germany, United Kingdom and Sweden

Government policy on the family in Germany, the United Kingdom and Sweden differs regarding to the degree of public funding and ideology. Public funding for family policy is strong in Germany and Sweden, in contrast to the UK where the cost of children is viewed primarily as the private business of parents. Individual parents can enjoy better provisions than the national average if they work for an employer who, as a result of negotiations, has conceded better provisions during childbearing such as longer/ (better) paid parental leaves and/or provide daycare for children of employees. Although there is stronger government involvement in family policies both in Germany and Sweden, the ideology differs in that Germany promotes one earner/one carer families, which implies financial benefits for the breadwinner and little help to combine work and family. Swedish policies, on the other hand, promote equal role sharing within the family. (See Chapter 2 for more details). A summary of family policies is given in Table 6.1.

Table 6.1: Family Policies in Germany, Great Britain and Sweden

	Germany	Great Britain	Sweden
Maternity and Parental leave			
Job protection	36 mths	6.7 mths	18 mths
Parental benefits	90% of earnings 6 weeks at maximum; DM 600/month, 6 months thereafter means tested	90% of earnings, 6 weeks £30, 12 weeks	75% of earnings, 15 mths
Child benefit	DM 200/month, 1st and 2nd chld DM 300/m 3rd+	£ 10/w ± DM 90/m 1st chld ± DM 70/m 2nd+	SEK 750/m ± DM 170 all
Child care	kindergarten 64% of age 3-6 9% full day	private	Public daycare 51% 0-2 ± 60% 3-5 full day
Taxation			
Taxation regime	Joint tax for couples since 1948	Couples taxed as individuals since 1991	Couples taxed as individuals since 1971
Basic allowance adults transferable	DM 5616	£ 1720 ± DM 3800	None
Adults non transferable	No	£ 3445 ± DM 7700	SEK 10 000 ± DM 2200
Child allowance	DM 6264	None	None

Parental leave and benefits

Paid maternity leave will reduce direct wage loss to the mother (w_t in relation (2)) if the woman leaves the the labour market. However, the loss of human capital investment will be greater the longer the period of leave. The longest job guarantee period is to be found in Germany, where jobs are guaranteed for 24 months after childbirth for most of our observation period, since 1993 increased to 36 months. Sweden combines a rather long job protection period of 18 months with relatively high levels of pay compensation. Until January 1996, new mothers were entitled to maternity benefits equalling 90% of earnings for the first 12 months. The current (1997) regulation is 10 months with 75% for either parent and one month with 90% compensation for the father if he chooses to take parental leave and one month with 90% compensation for the mother. In addition, three months are compensated at a flat rate for either the father or mother. A

Swedish woman therefore has an incentive to have a job first and a child next, since having no earnings before childbearing means that she gets only a small guarantee benefit.

Effective from 1986, a second child born within 30 months of the first entitles the mother to parental leave benefit based on her earnings before the birth of her first child in Sweden. This policy referred to in the literature as the 'speed premium', developed as mothers whose children were born in quick succession brought cases to the Swedish National Insurance Board claiming that the births were so close that it was impossible to earn similar income between births. The 'speed premium' is widely chosen as many as 40% of Swedish mothers of two or more children have their second child within 30 months (Hoem, 1993). of course the profitability of a strategy of one career interruption rather than two will depend on a number of factors: the length of the interruptions; income compensation during parental leave; the women's human capital accumulation function; and whether any depreciation effects occur that count for lower wages than a loss of human capital investment in itself. However, this 'speed premium' is a policy instrument if one deems close spacing to be politically desirable, which it might be if the medical concerns of late births are at all important. In Sweden however the speed premium resulted from the effects on income of parents who happened to have a close spacing of childbirths. It has since become a decision parameter for prospective parents.

In the other countries parental leave and benefits after the first born are also extended if the second child is born in the job protection period, but benefits are paid only during a short period and are lower than in Sweden. Therefore the other countries do not give a 'speed premium' to mothers in order to space their children in a short period.

Unlike the Swedish paid parental leave, German parental leave subsidy is not related to previous earnings except for a period of two months following the birth (Athe Mutterschutz' period). Currently the mother who cares full-time for her child and refrains from paid labour receives 600 DM per month for 24 months unless her husband has a high income, in which case she may lose the 'Erziehungsgeld' after the seventh month of the job guarantee period. The parental leave subsidy becomes means-tested against family income from the seventh month (Ostner 1993: 102). In addition, Germany has child benefits that increase in line with the number of children (Zimmermann, 1993:210) and tax deductions based on the number of children (Zimmermann, 1993:208). Career-oriented women confronted with German long-leave provisions, but low or no pay compensation may be more eager to return to the labour market even before the job guarantee period has expired because they face both a higher wage loss and a higher human capital loss. However Ondrich, Spiess and Yang (1996) show that German women have been making use of the longer job protection periods as these have gradually been extended.

Introduced in 1986 at 10 months, the job protection period in Germany for women having a child was extended to twelve months in 1988, to 18 months in 1990, to 24 months in 1992 and to 36 months in 1993 (Zimmermann 1993). There is reason to believe that career-oriented women are well informed about their potential human capital loss and know that the loss will be smaller towards the end of their careers. In Germany economic incentives to have a job first and a child next in order to protect the labour market attachment and (higher) maternity benefits during home child caring time, is smaller than in Sweden but the importance of a job protection period should not be underestimated in facilitating the return to work. Albrecht et al (1996) shed an interesting light on the career break effect of parental leave on wages of mothers in Sweden. A number of studies using US data indicate that time out of the labour market has a negative impact on women's wages which exceeds the effect of lost experience i.e. depreciation of human capital. In cross section specifications for Sweden (Albrecht et al, 1996), they confirmed expectations that job interruptions adversely affect women's wages, but time used for parental leave during the job protection period did not result in reduced wages. Depreciation of human capital is found to occur during periods of unemployment and periods out of the labour market which exceed the job protection period.

Britain's legal job guarantee period (6.7 months in 1996) and period of maternity benefits (18 weeks in 1996) are very small compared to those in Germany and Sweden. The British case approximates the situation which would arise in the absence of public policies and shows similarities with results of US studies. For Britain, Ni Bhrolchain (1983, 1985a) and Martin & Roberts (1984) found that in Britain return time to work after the birth of the latest child was strongly linked to prior interbirth working. Women who returned to work within five years after giving birth to their last child were two to three times as likely as others to have worked between their first and last child.

Childcare

In addition to benefits during the parental leave period and job protection, the availability and cost of good quality childcare are important in combining paid work and family. In all three countries childcare provision for children under three is less than ideal. Swedish policy is that children in their first year of life should be cared for exclusively by their parents, which is supported by generous paid parental leave. There is little childcare available for children younger than 18 months. In 1988 roughly 90% of Swedish children under the age of one were exclusively cared for by their parents who were on paid parental leave (SCB 1989). However, for children from about four years onwards there is now in Sweden 'full needs supply' (full behovstäckning) of day-care. Parents' contributions to the costs of public day-care in Sweden are mostly income-linked and averaged less than 10% of total costs for the entire period 1975-1990 (Gustafsson and Stafford, 1992). In 1994 they had increased to 13.4% (Socialstyrelsen 1995).

In Germany there is little all-day childcare although in 1990 some 65% of German children aged three to six had a place in local government subsidised good quality kindergartens which are part-day (Zimmermann 1993). Combining children with full-time work in Germany is also more difficult because most schools are organised with morning lessons ending at 1 pm on the assumption that children will be helped with schoolwork at home.

In Great Britain public provision of day care is extremely limited apart from pre-primary education lasting several hours a day. In contrast to Sweden but similar to German kindergartens, working mothers are not given priority. As a result British mothers- like their German counterparts who wish to combine work and family- are forced to rely on ad hoc arrangements and the informal sector. (Sainsbury 1996).

Income tax

Because they are taxed separately, Swedish wives have an economic incentive to increase their working hours relative to their husbands. This contrasts with German wives whose earnings are added to those of their husband before taxation. Consequently a part-time job contributes relatively more to family income in Sweden, because the small incomes of part-time working wives are taxed at lower rates than the larger incomes of full-time working husbands (Gustafsson 1992). Whereas in Germany part-time earnings are taxed on top of husbands earnings, Great Britain occupies a place between the German split-taxation system and the Swedish individual tax system, utilising one transferable basic deduction which is an element of joint taxation, and one non-transferable basic deduction which is an element of separate taxation. The relatively large personal non-transferable deduction in Great Britain represents an incentive to work short hours and earn an income small enough to be within the limits of the personal deduction, to avoid any taxation at all. However such jobs are often ineligible for any type of social security benefit and are often low skilled, dead end jobs.

Conclusion: hypotheses to be posited from family policies

The review of family policies in this section shows that, compared to Germany and Sweden, Great Britain implements few if any policies that modify the market mechanisms governing women's choices. As such the considerations set out in section 2 remain valid. Highly productive women who care both about their paid careers and their families will tend to postpone the birth of their first child but it will make no difference to them whether they space their children around a single career break or they return to work in between children as long as the total career break is of a given duration. Less productive women will be less in a hurry to return to work and also less in a hurry to have a second child. In Sweden we may expect fewer differences between more productive women and less productive women because of policies to combine work and family. In addition the so-called 'speed premium' makes clustering of births a profitable option which should distinguish Swedish women's behaviour from behaviour in the other two countries. In Germany the combination of work and family is not facilitated by social policies, rather the contrary. The incentive for highly productive women to postpone births is therefore strong. Once the first child has been born, a rapid return to paid work is unlikely because of the long job protection period. German women considering spacing their children close together rather than two shorter career interruptions are not influenced by public policies and should therefore be indifferent between the two choices. Because Germany favours full-time maternal care rather than assisting mothers to combine work with family, there could be a demarcation line between the highly productive women who want to combine work and family and others who do not wish or cannot struggle against the 'male breadwinner' organisation of the German society. Individual human capital considerations will be more important in Germany than in Sweden.

Data and comparability of variable definitions across countries

This chapter makes use of the German Socio Economic Panel (GSOEP, 1983-1992, annual surveys) the Swedish Household Market and Nonmarket Activities Panel (HUS, 1984-1993, surveys every second year and spell data) and the British Household Panel Survey (BHPS, 1990-1992, retrospective data from 1980). We organised the data sets with date of birth of a child in the household as a starting point. Some births during our observation period are first births, some are second births and some are third births. The surveys contain information on human capital variables, earnings and hours worked of the mother and her spouse. The variable monthly changes in labour market status around childbirth has been defined in the different surveys in the following way.

In HUS, maternity leave can be separated only in the survey year and not in the month-to-month spell data files. In the spell data it is included under 'being on leave', which category also comprises sick leave, vacation, absence from work. In GSOEP maternity leave becomes a separate category of labour force status from the 1988 survey. To arrive at a variable of women on maternity leave before 1988 we used the information on women who chose 'other' as their labour force status and matched some other criteria.

Changes in labour force status in the British Household Panel Survey (BHPS) is available from retrospective information (1980-1990). Since the British data are retrospective, women were asked to give the birth dates of all their children, whereas in the Swedish and German panel data only births that occurred during the observation period were included. British respondents had to cover a 10 year period retrospectively and give information on labour force status for each month during each of these 10 years. However no earnings data are collected because it is impossible to remember earnings retrospectively. In the annual surveys from 1990 onwards the BHPS collects earnings data but there are no earnings data for earlier years. For the definitions and comparability of the variables on education and years of experience see Chapter 2.

For husband's pre-tax earnings in Sweden we used the response to the following question that was asked in all surveys: 'How much do you earn, before taxes at your primary job?'. In the 1991 wave information was requested for 1989 and 1990. To supplement for missing information 'income from employment last year was used in connection with hours of work per week in the year under study. For Germany we used

Arbeitsverdienst brutto letzter Monat' including paid overtime work plus other benefits but excluding vacation benefits which is asked in all yearly surveys. The following survey year the GSOEP includes a question on vacation benefits last year, but since there are many missing on this variable we did not include it. We have recomputed earnings for both countries into 1993 prices and used the purchasing power parity of 1993, which is one DM equals 4.71 SEK (OECD, 1995).

Who postpones first birth?

Tables 6.2 and 6.3 shows number of women included in our samples by birth order and number of births and by age at birth of the first child respectively. Table 6.3 shows the mean age of the mother at first birth computed from the micro panel data. There are some common characteristics for all three countries. First, in all three countries more highly educated women tend to have their first child at a later age than their less educated women.

Secondly, women who proceed later to have another child have had their first child earlier in life than women who are observed only to have had a first birth. This pattern is true within each educational group and across educational groups for all three countries, except for more highly educated Swedish women. Also the women who were observed to have three children in the data had their first child at a still younger age than those who were observed to have two children. If we had been observing completed fertility spells rather than data censored at the interview date, age at first birth of those women who have only one child during lifetime might have been still higher. This is because some women will have more children after our observation period.

Comparing our three countries we observe some consistent differences. Women in Great Britain become mothers at a younger age than either in Germany or in Sweden. This is true for all subgroups presented in Table 6.3. In Great Britain because benefits are small less educated women have less reason to think about earning a right to a maternity benefit than is the case in Germany and Sweden. This may lead to earlier motherhood among less educated British women in comparison to German and Swedish women. However as in the other two countries, more highly educated wo-

Table 6.2: Women Included in our Samples by Number of Births and Birth Order

	West Germany	Great Britain	Sweden
Only first child observed	283	355	59
only second child	111	a	51
only third child	52	a	50
first & second child	157	440	60
Second & third child	34	a	19
First, second & third child	28	139	8
Number of women	665	934	247

Data: GSOEP(1983-1992), BHPS (1990-1992, retrospective 1980-) & HUS (1984-1993)
a)= not applicable. Because the British data relies on retrospective information on births: there are no cases of whom we have only information on e.g. 2nd birth.

Table 6.3: Age at First Birth, of Women Included in our Samples

	West Germany	Great Britain	Sweden
only 1st birth in data	27.32	25.98	27.89
1st and 2nd birth in data	26.07	24.77	26.77
1st, 2nd & 3rd birth in data	24.26	22.41	-
Higher education			
Only 1st birth in data	29.3	27.3	29.6
1st and 2nd birth in data	28.4	27.2	30.2
1st, 2nd & 3rd birth in data	25.8	24.6	-
Lower education			
Only 1st birth in data	26.6	25.4	27.1
1st and 2nd birth in data	25.3	24.1	26.6
1st, 2nd & 3rd birth in data	23.7	21.9	-

Data: GSOEP(1983-1992), BHPS (1990-1992, retrospective 1980-)& HUS (1984-1993); Proportion of highly educated in West-German sample:27.3; in Great Britain 23.2 and in Sweden 28.9. For Sweden only 8 obs. for 1st, 2nd & 3rd, so it is not reported. Higher education corresponds to having completed "Abitur" in Germany, having completed "Studentexamen" in Sweden and having completed "A-level" in Great Britain.

men in Britain have to consider their labour market prospects and this induces postponement of motherhood as explained in section 2 above. The relatively brief job guarantee period in Britain might make having a child more costly in career terms than would be the case if the job protection period was larger because a mother may have to give up her job and find a new one before she can return to paid employment. Consequently British women are forced to pay more attention to the career costs of having children. On the other hand, British women by contrast to Swedish women do not have to build up a right to maternity benefits. The lower age at maternity in Britain compared to Sweden and Germany to same degree can be explained by the fact that the British data cover the period from 1980 whereas the German data start in 1983 and the Swedish start in 1984. Demographic trends in all three countries have shown a rise in the age of first-time mothers over time, which works in the direction of younger mothers in Great Britain where the period 1980-1982 is included.

Econometric analysis of mother's age at first birth

Using information from our theoretical considerations and the likely impact of differences in government policies on the family in the three countries surveyed, we now proceed to examine mother's age at first birth in each country. One of our theoretical predictions of Section 2 implies that other things equal, the higher husband's income, the earlier the birth of the first child. The theoretical variable for the influence of husband's income is the present value of his life-time earnings which is not available. Therefore we use predicted income at age 40 following Willis (1973) for the Swedish and the German data for which we have information on husband's income at the birth of the first child and his age at this point in time. We compute predicted income at age 40 of the husband by estimating age earnings functions of the form:

$$(4)\ \ln(y)^b = \beta_0 + \beta_1 S^b + \beta_2 age^b + \beta_3 (age^b)^2 + E^b$$

where y is the monthly income of the husband at childbirth, S^b the husband's years of education at time of birth and his age at birth. E^b is the error term, also measured at birth. Income at age 40 is then computed by moving husband's income to his 40th birthday along the estimated age-earnings curve while assuming that his education remains constant. Predicted income at age 40 is then computed by using the parameters estimated by (4) above and the difference between husband's actual age at birth and age 40, as follows:

$$(5) \quad pred. \ \ln(y40) = \hat{\beta}_0 + \hat{\beta}_1 S^b + \hat{\beta}_2 age^b + \hat{\beta}_2 (40 - age^b) + \hat{\beta}_3 (age^b)^2 + \hat{\beta}_3 (40 - age^b)^2 + E^b$$

where β_i : i=0..3 are taken from (4) and superscript b means at time of birth of the child. For Great Britain we have no information on husbands' income at the time of their child(ren)'s birth. Instead we use a variable on the husband's occupational status, according to a 7 categories scale with 7 being the most prestigious occupational group.[48]

Table 6.4 shows the results. We present three regressions per country. The first regression includes only mother's characteristics, the second regression includes in addition husband's income at age 40 and the third regression includes both husband's income at age 40 and his schooling. The effect of husband's income at age 40 on the timing of motherhood is positive and statistically significant for Sweden which means that the higher husband's income, the later first birth – which is contrary to the predictions by economic theory.[49] For Germany we do not find a significant effect of husband's income on the timing of first birth. The variable husband's schooling is meant to capture his education and career planning and we find that there is an effect independent of income,[50] for Germany and Great Britain, but not for Sweden. In Britain first births are timed later the higher the husband's level of education and the higher his positioning on a seven-step occupational ladder. For all three countries we found that when husband's income and education are held constant, the more well-educated the woman the longer she postpones motherhood. To sum up the results of Table 6.4, we do not find the expected impact from a husband's income but we find the expected effect on timing of maternity of mother's level of education. The impact of having more than one child is also as expected (except for the second birth in Sweden). We also

---

[48]   The regressions for Great-Britian on the one hand and Germany and Sweden on the other hand are not fully comparable because the income variable is not available for Britain. This might lead to omitted variable bias, if for example the income of the spouse is correlated with the educational level of the woman.

[49]   This is in line with results for The Netherlands by W. Groot and H. Pott-Buter (1992) analysing OSA 1980-1985.

[50]   Since husband's education is used to predict husband's income, there is multi collinearity. However running the regressions including both income and education does performs better than the regressions excluding husband's education. This means that husband's schooling has an independent effect.

Table 6.4: OLS on Timing of First Birth in West Germany, Sweden and Great Britain (dep. var: age of the mother)

	West Germany			Sweden			Great Britain		
Const.	26.921	26.542	21.213	25.978	20.059	19.098	25.388	23.079	22.171
	(103.4)	(62.37)	(23.94)	(50.97)	(9.44)	(8.79)	(92.71)	(28.80)	(18.11)
education mother at 1st birth=high[b]	3.351	2.964	1.564	4.074	4.00	3.578	3.651	2.201	2.210
	(5.71)	(4.44)	(2.28)	(6.84)	(6.44)	(5.64)	(7.81)	(4.27)	(3.69)
second birth=1	-1.038	-1.267	-1.252	-0.458	-0.297	-0.511	-1.040	-1.621	-1.452
	(-3.35)	(-2.95)	(-3.04)	(-0.80)	(-0.49)	(-0.86)	(-2.95)	(-3.8)	(-3.06)
third birth=1	-1.470	-1.817	-1.991	-3.09	-3.03	-3.226	-2.348	-2.06	-1.99
	(-1.91)	(-2.31)	(-2.64)	(-4.98)	(-4.76)	(-5.08)	(-5.43)	(-4.00)	(-3.43)
income husband at age 40		0.180	-0.030		0.350	0.296		0.248	0.119
		(1.45)	(0.24)		(2.82)	(2.56)		(3.00)	(1.03)
schooling spouse			0.0478			0.210			0.310
			(5.81)			(1.56)			(3.40)
Rsq	0.26	0.09	0.17	0.40	0.24	0.26	0.12	0.14	0.15
N	465	395	395	99	87	87	844	535	535

Data: Germany: GSOEP 1983-1993, West-Germans. Great Britain: Sweden HUS 1984-1993. BHPS 1990-1992 and retrospective data 1980-1991. N=number of observations. We have less observations than presented in Table 6.1 because information on the spouse as age and education is missing. a) BHPS has no information on earnings: we used information on occupational status of the spouse: 1=not in job,2=unskilled,3=partly skilled,4=skilled manual,5=skilled nonmanual,6=managerial&technical,7=professional; b)Education is high: >=12 years of schooling.

performed regressions for the husband's actual income at child birth for Germany and Sweden, which showed the same effects. The regressions including a dummy variable equal to one if the mother is observed ever to have returned to the labour market after her first child (not presented in Table 6.4) was not significant for Great Britain and Germany whereas for Sweden it shows the expected sign implying that career-oriented mothers have their first child later in life.

Clustering births or second career break?

In this section we address the question on how women time their re-entry into the labour market after their first child and between subsequent births. Table 6.5 shows a cross-tabulation of the number of months elapsed since the first child before the mother enters the labour force according to how many births women have had and whether they returned to the labour market between children. The data is first divided into three groups: A. women for whom only first birth are observed in the data; B. women for whom first and second births are observed; and C. women for whom we observe first, second and third births. For women who have more than one child the data is further divided according to whether the women returned to paid employment between births or not. A further distinction is made between labour force participation in part-time work or in full-time work. Not surprisingly we find that the period out of employment is longer when mothers choose not to re-enter the labour market between births than if there is a spell of paid work between births. This is clear by comparing columns (2) and (4) and columns (4) and (5) respectively. The time it takes before entering into paid work is not influenced by whether the woman enters into part-time or full-time employment. This is true for both Germany and Sweden. In both countries a large majority of mothers choose part-time employment rather than full-time employment. This is true for 139 out of 220 mothers, i.e. 63% across categories in Germany and for 66 out of 75 observations i.e. 75% in Sweden. For Great-britian the data does not allow to make this distinction. Swedish mothers are assisted in this choice by family policies because parents have a legal right to shorten work hours to six hours a day until their child is eight years old, and then return to full-time in the same job. The employer cannot refuse a mother or in more rare cases a father the six hour work day and also not refuse a mother or a father to increase work hours again when their child is eight years old.

This daily reduction in working hours is at the cost of the employee and effectively amounts to two hours unpaid leave a day.

One interesting similarity across countries in Table 6.5 is that women who enter the labour market between births do so after about 12 months in all three countries, although the job protection period varies between countries. This might lead one to posit a biologically and emotionally optimum of 12 months full-time baby care coupled with a subsequent return to work on a part-time basis. One difference between Sweden and the other two countries is that a greater proportion of Swedish first time mothers re-enter the labour market between first and second births: 35% in Germany and 39% in Great Britain compared to 47% in Sweden., which can be seen by taking the observations on those who do return as a proportion of all mothers who have at least two births in our data.

Sweden also differs from the other two countries in that the duration of time out of the labour market is not longer for the women for whom we observe only the first child than for women who re-enter between births i.e. 12 to 14 months. In Germany and Britain only first birth mothers wait 17 to 22 months. For women who do not re-enter between births in Sweden and Germany the duration of home time is between 43-49 months i.e. three and a half to five years. In Great Britain, on the other hand, those who do not re-enter between the first and the second birth have a spell of home time of some 58 to 65 months i.e. around five years.

Months elapsed between first and second birth and between second and third births presented in the lower part of Table 6.5 show that these periods are quite similar between the three countries, and therefore we can compare the period of return to work between countries quite well.

Tables 6.6 and 6.7 show proportional hazard regressions on the time spent before entering the labour force after the birth of a first child and the timing of a second birth. However these two regressions do not really capture our theoretical model, which says that a highly economically productive mother is indifferent as to whether she has a second child relatively quickly with one career interruption or re-enters the labour market between births and delays the second child. Are women, who are highly productive (have a high β in equation (2)) more in a hurry to pursue one of the two options than women who are less productive? A more

Table 6.5:   Number of Months since First Birth before Entering Employment

Births in data	A: only 1st	B: 1st & 2nd birth		C. 1st, 2nd & 3rd birth	
Mother enters	After 1st birth	Between 1st & 2nd birth	Only after 2nd birth	Between 1st & 2nd birth	Only after 2nd birth
		mean (st dev) and number of observations			
W-Germany					
Full-time or part-time	21.3 124 (19.2)	12.7 5 (8.3)	47.4 14 (47.4)	11.4 12 (5.7)	43.6 5 (24.7)
In full-time	20.3 43 (20.6)	12.1 2 (9.1)	43.0 5 (12.4)	13.8 8 (5.7)	46.0 3 (25.5)
In part-time	21.8 81 (18.6)	13.1 4 (8.0)	49.9 9 (17.2)	7.8 4 (7.8)	40.0 2 (14.1)
Great Britain					
Full-time or part-time	17.1 133 (21.3)	12.0 135 (12.6)	58.4 78 (29.1)	7.9 32 (5.9)	65.0 2 (30.9)
Sweden					
Full-time or part-time	14.4 36 (10.3)	13.0 9 (6.6)	45.7 7 (18.7)	12.5 7 (6.4)	44.8 4 (20.6)
In full-time	12.4 5 (5.4)	14.1 15 (8.5)	59 1	-	36.0 1
In part-time	14.7 31 (10.9)	12.3 24 (5.1)	43.5 6 (19.4)	12.5 2 (6.4)	47.7 3 (4.2)
Months elapsed between 1st and 2nd birth (mean, n) Return is fulltime or part time					
W- Germany		38.4 65	24.5 14	32.6 12	19.2 5
Great Britain		40.4 135	24.3 78	34.5 32	22.3 42
Sweden		32.0 39	23.4 7	22.0 2	23.0 4
Months elapsed between 2nd and 3rd birth (mean, n). Return is fulltime or part time					
W-Germany				27.5 2	33.0 5
Great Britain				33.4 32	39.4 42
Sweden				37.0 2	21.6 4

Data: Germany: GSOEP 1983-1993, West-Germans. Great Britain: BHPS 1990-1992 and retrospective data 1980-1991. Sweden HUS 1984-1993. For Britain we are not able to split timing of return to work in full-time and part-time. Full-time means 35 hours work per week or more.

Table 6.6:   **Proportional Hazards of Months before Entering the Labour Force after First Birth in Connection with a Subsequent Birth, all First Time Mothers**

	West Germany	Sweden	Great Britain
Age of the mother at 1st birth	-0.087	-0.039	-0.059
	(-2.47)	(-0.81)	(-2.82)
Schooling of the mother at 1st birth	0.098	-0.009	0.112
	(2.52)	(-0.19)	(4.19)
employment experience of the mother at 1st birth	0.072	0.035	0.716
	(2.33)	(0.65)	(3.50)
husband's income before taxes at 1st birth	-0.055	0.114	
	(-1.16)	(1.09)	
subsequent child	-0.669	-0.114	0.233
	(-4.08)	(-0.46)	(2.57)
LogL	-862.1	-447.97	-5.280.2
N	438	125	1381

Data: Germany: GSOEP 1983-1993, West-Germans. Great Britain: BHPS 1990-1992 and retrospective data 1980-1991. Sweden HUS 1984-1993.

Table 6.7:   **Proportional Hazards of Months before having a Second Child after the First Birth in Connection with Participating in the Labour Force after the First Birth, all First Time Mothers**

	West Germany	Sweden	Great Britain
Age of the mother at 1st birth	-0.050	-0.055	-0.068
	(-1.60)	(-0.81)	(-2.86)
Schooling of the mother at 1st birth	0.010	0.014	0.058
	(0.24)	(0.20)	(1.80)
Employment experience of the mother at 1st birth	-0.021	0.046	0.042
	(-2.33)	(0.63)	(1.80)
husband's income before taxes at 1st birth	0.111	0.194	
	(2.13)	(1.64)	
Participating after the 1st birth=yes	-0.802	-0.291	-0.646
	(-4.55)	(-4.42)	(-6.84)
LogL	-722.3	-259.86	-3.304.5
N	507	103	1137

Data: Germany: GSOEP 1983-1993, West-Germans. Great Britain: BHPS 1990-1992 and retrospective data 1980-1991. Sweden HUS 1984-1993.

adquate model would be a competing risk model. We have tried to estimate such a model but with no success.[51]

In Table 6.6. we take account of the possible effect that a second birth has on the timing of entering the labour market after the first birth by specifying a variable in the proportional hazard which is time varying and indicates whether a second child is born and when the second child is born. In Table 6.6. this variable is labelled subsequent child. When we observe in our data that a woman gives birth to a subsequent birth we have two observations of this woman in our data, if we do not observe a subsequent child we have one observation of the woman. By observing the woman who gives birth to a subsequent child twice we test whether a subsequnet child improves her hazard or not. As expected having a subsequent child delays entering the labour market after giving birth to the first child in Germany and Sweden. In Britain on the other hand having a subsequent child seems to increase the speed of entering the labour market after first birth.

Table 6.6 indicates that in Germany and Great Britain the younger the mother is at the birth of the first child the less eager she is to enter paid employment afterwards. In Table 6.6 we also find that in Germany and Great Britain, women with more human capital accumulated at time of first birth spend less time at home since both education of the mother and years of experience of the mother have a positive effect on the number of months before entering paid employment. This effect is in line to our expectations that women with more human capital should be more eager to return to paid work.

As in Table 6.6 we included in the proportional hazard model presented in Table 6.7 a time varying variable indicating whether a woman entered the labour market after giving birth to the first child to test whether this affects the timing of the second birth. As expected we find that if the mother enters paid work after the first birth it takes her longer to have a second childbirth than if she does not re-enter employment after first birth. This is true for all three countries. In Germany a woman who has a longer employment history prior to motherhood waits longer before having a

---

[51]   These attempts were carried out in cooperation with Hans van Ophem at the University of Amsterdam, who has himself developed and estimated such models (see e.g. Ophem and Jonk, 1997). None of our model specifications resulted in any statistically significant or interpretable results.

second child. If the husband's income is larger, the woman will wait for a shorter period before having a second child.

Conclusions

This chapter indicates that women become mothers later if husbands' incomes are higher which is contrary to our expectations. When women have more than one child eventually-born, they become mothers earlier. First births occur later the higher the mother's and father's respective levels of education, which is in line with the expectations raised by economic theory set out in this chapter. In a cross tabulation study we find a striking similarity between all three countries in that it takes about a year before a mother returns to work if she does return at all before having a second child. In our proportional hazard estimate of months before re-entry into the labour market we find that women in Germany and Britain with a larger degree of human capital wait shorter to return to work than women with a smaller amount of human capital. This result is in line with our hypothesis.

7 Optimal Age at Maternity in The Netherlands

There was not one amongst us who looked forward to being born. We disliked the rigours of existence, the unfulfilled longings, the enshrined injustices of the world, the labyrinths of love, the ignorance of parents, the fact of dying, and the amazing indifference of the Living in the midst of the simple beauties of the universe. We feared the heartlessness of human beings all of whom are born blind, few of whom ever learn to see.
The Famished Road, Ben Okri, 1992:3.

Introduction

In The Netherlands the mean age at which women give birth to their first child started to increase in the 1970s from 24.3 years in 1970 to 28.9 years in 1996 (Statistics Netherlands 1994, 1998). According to statistics of the Council of Europe (1996) Dutch women give birth to their first child at a later age than 31 other European countries from 1980 onwards. In 1994 the mean age of Dutch women at maternity was 28.4 years compared to 27.9 years for former West Germany, 27.2 years for Sweden, 26.6 years for former East Germany and 26.5 years for England and Wales.[52] The proportion of first-time mothers who were 35 years or older in The Netherlands increased from 3.4 in 1985 to 9.1% in 1995 (Statistics Netherlands,1985,1-997). Biomedical risks increase with postponement of childbearing,

---

[52] The countries included in the Council of Europe (1996) are: Austria, Belgium, Bulgaria, Cyprus, Czech Republic, Denmark Estonia, Finland, France, Germany, Greece, Hungary, Iceland, Ireland, Italy, Latvia, Lithuania, The Netherlands, Norway, Poland, Portugal, Romania, San Marino, Slovac Republic, Slovenia, Spain, Sweden, Switzerland, Republic of Macedonia, Turkey, United Kingdom. Another study by Bosveld (1996) showing the age at which 75% of the cohort women born in 1955 had their first child. West Germany is the highest in this ranking: 33.8 years. Second is The Netherlands: 32.8 years.

especially after the age of 35. These risks not only lead to health and psychological personal costs when the woman and/or her spouse turn out not to be as fertile as they expected to be, but they also result in medical[53] and other societal costs. Postponement of the first birth may also increase biomedical risks relating to subsequent births.

Van Luijn (1996) analysing Dutch women in the age category 20-40 years shows that reasons for postponement and refrainment of children are related to not being able to have a combination of children and 'other personal development' such as a labour market career. De Beer (1997) analyses the probability of ever having a child among women 34 to 43 years old in 1993 according to three levels of education. The sample is split into women who live with a man and those who do not. For women who do not live with a man the expectation to ever give birth to a child differs very much according to education. Among the highly educated single women more than half (57%) expect never to have a child, among the medium educated single women the corresponding figure is 33% and among the low educated single women it is 20%. For those who do live with a man the expectations of never giving birth according to education are 24%, 11% and 10% for high, medium and low educated women respectively.

Dutch women have invested in their earnings capacity increasingly during the last decade. Young women's attained educational level is comparable to men's in 1996[54] (ROA [Researchcentrum voor Onderwijs en Arbeidsmarkt] Research Centre for Education and the Labour Market,1997),

---

[53] For example, 1 out of 100 births per year (the total number of live births in 1995 :190,500) in The Netherlands are born out of In Vitro Fertilization (IVF) (Fauser, 1998), which costs directly amounted to Dfl 33 mln in 1991 (Bonsel en Van der Maas, 1994). The chance on successful treatment decreases with age at treatment (Bouwens, 1996). For women below age 30 the chance on successful IVF treatment is14%, for women between 35 and 39 the probability of a life birth due to IVF is 7%. The mean age at IVF treatment in The Netherlands is 34 years (Leerentveld, 1993).
  If we only consider the direct medical costs connected with postponement of children that mostly strike the eye, like costs of pro-fertility treatments, diagnoses of complications/handicaps, additional echoscopes, caesarian sections, and intensive care costs for early births (pre births) in hospital then these costs amounted to Dfl 700 million in 1991.
  Additional health complications and additional medical and social care (time) for the woman before conception, during pregnancy and after delivery, plus health and social problems of the child is not taken into account.
[54] However the gender role pattern in educational field persists in that men mainly choose technical fields and women mainly choose fields leading to careers in care (CPB 1997, ROA 1997).

and during the last decade women's labour force participation rates increased. In all national labour market scenarios until 2020 (Central Planning Bureau CPB/Statistics Netherlands, 1997) a further increase in women's labour force participation is assumed,[55] particularly for women aged 30-54 years. Full-time employment dominates in the rest of Europe but in The Netherlands there is more part-time employment than in any other European country.

Almost 90% of Dutch women and men in the age categories 18-42 would like to have children (Statistics Netherlands, 1994). In the period when their children are born and shortly thereafter most parents do not prefer to have two full-time jobs. In the planning of timing of birth the couple has to consider financial consequences as well as their wish to have time for the care of their child. There is also pleasure derived as well from the care of the child as from market work. Family policies like parental leaves and enough affordable child care facilities of good quality, have an influence on this timing decision.

It is not possible to exactly determine the end of a woman's fertile period (Fauser, 1998), but in general the biologically optimal time period of having children is between 18 and 35. This period coincides with the period in a woman's life when it is optimal to devote time to work and human capital investment.

We analyse the optimal age of giving birth considering career costs for women who would like to have both children and a career, by studying the shape of the potential age earnings curve. In principle, it might be optimal to give birth at a point in time when costs in terms of human capital investments forgone have decreased. The optimization problem is to minimize the sum of direct wage loss and the accumulated return to human capital investments forgone, subject to the desired time out for childbearing and infant care.

---

[55]   Three scenarios of the future development of Dutch labour supply are based on alternative assumptions on future changes in the population and changes in labour force participation rates. In the next 25 years four developments will definitely have an influence on the labour force in 2020. Aging of society, the flattening of the increase of the average educational level, the increasing number of ethnic minorities and the increase of women's labour force particpation. The labor force participation rate (lfp) of women aged 20-64 is assumed to be in the three scenarios: 58% (demographic growth low & economic growth low, 63% (demographic growth medium, economic growth high) and 60% (demographic growth high, economic growth medium) in 2010; and 68%, 77% and 74% in 2020. The lfp of men is assumed to remain about 80% in all three scenarios.

We use the Dutch micro panel data on labour market behaviour of households (OSA, 1985-1996) which includes wages and information on investments in human capital for persons, and their relationships within households. We use the most recent wave of OSA (1996) to analyse potential age earnings curves for the planning problem of timing of maternity. In addition we use the OSA waves in 1985-1996 for women and their spouses who have their first child during the period 1985-1996 (see Chapter 3).

The outline of this chapter is as follows. First we present some results of earlier Dutch studies on the connection between women's labour force participation and childbearing. Secondly we present theoretical considerations concerning timing of births from an economic perspective. Thirdly we discuss what the relevant age earnings standard is for the potential career of a woman. Next, we present simulations of life time earnings loss at different points in life for different educational levels. Finally we present conclusions.

Women's education, labour force participation, hours of work and fertility

The trend of increasing postponement of maternity occurred simultaneously with increasing educational attainment of women and increasing labour force participation rates in The Netherlands. De Beer (Statistics Netherlands, 1997) shows that less than 20% of the women born towards the end of the 1950s were in full time education at age 20, while of the women born in the 1970s, 40% were in full-time education at age 20.

The Dutch Institute called Organisatie voor Strategisch Arbeidsmarktonderzoek (OSA) publishes a study on labour force participation and other labour market characteristics based on each wave of the OSA survey. The labour force participation rates in these studies include jobs with less than 12 hours. Comparing the year 1988 (OSA, Allaart et al. 1991) to the year 1996 (OSA, Kunnen et al. 1997) labour force participation of all women increased from 44.2% to 58.5%.[56] Women who do not (yet) have children, have labour force participation rates similar to those of men. While 86.2% of childless women (mean age:30.0) were employed and 5.1% were self employed, for childless men (mean age:31.3) the figures were 85.4 % employed and 7.3% self employed (OSA, Kunnen et al. 1997).

---

[56]   For women with children below the age of 6 the increase was very large, namely, from 26% in 1988 to 57% in 1996 (OSA, 1997).

Labour force participation rates differ according to educational level. In 1996 women with higher vocational training or university degree (highly educated) have a labour force participation rate of 74.0%, while women with less education have a labour participation rate of 50.7%. There is no difference in labour force participation rates between educational groups for women who are (yet) childless. The employment rate of both groups is around 83 and around 8% are self employed. However, the labour force participation rates of women with at least one child below the age of 6 differ according to educational level. For the higher educated women within this group, the labour force participation rate is 78%, but for the lower educated women within this group the labour force participation rate is 51% (OSA, Kunnen et al. 1997).

Although labour force participation rates increased over the last decade, the number of hours Dutch women supply to the labour market is still fairly low. Women who have children seldom work full-time, only 6% of married women who had a child younger than 11 years did so in comparison to childless women among whom full-time employment was 57.3% (Statistics Netherlands, 1996). Employed mothers who work more than 32 hours per week is 14%. The proportion of employed mothers who work 28 hours per week or more is 22.8.[57]

The small supply of hours to the market by women and especially by mothers, implies financial dependence. Van Berkel & De Graaf (1995) estimate that in 1991, 48.1% of Dutch married women are completely financially dependent on their husbands. Niphuis-Nell (1998) comments on this financial dependence that postponement of first birth gives the woman time to increase her equipment in the struggle to protect her economic position.

De Jong (1994) studies timing of first birth among women born during 1950-1954 and compares to the cohort born in 1960-1964. Women with higher education are considerably less likely to give birth before their 28th birth day. While 29% of women born between 1950-54 with higher education gave birth before age 28, the figure for less educated women was 73%. For the cohort of women born 10 years later the corresponding figures showed an increased tendency for both educational groups to delay childbirth. While only 16% of the highly educated women gave birth before

---

[57]   In 1996 the proportion of childless women working more than 32 hours per week is 62.7%. The proportion of employed childless women who work 28 hours per week or more is considerable higher: 84.6%. Own calculations on OSA (1996).

they were 28 years old, the figure for low educated women had decreased to 58%.

Theoretical considerations on optimal age at maternity

In this chapter we are interested in the planning problem of young women: when is the right time to give birth considering life time earnings? We intend to measure the direct costs and the human capital investments loss for different patterns of hours and participation during different lengths of labour market spells of women after having had their first child. Since women have different market productivity because of different educational attainment and different number of years of experience, the career costs differ by women's age at having their first child (as laid out in chapter 6).

Career costs consist on the one hand of direct loss of earnings due to leaving the labour market to give birth and care for a new born child and on the other hand the loss of returns until retirement because of human capital investments not undertaken during a period of home time.

The planning problem we want to analyse is depicted in Figure 7.1. The solid curve, her potential age earnings curve, w_0abc is the age earnings curve which the woman would face if she devotes all her energy full-time to the market career.

The actual age earnings curve of a mother will depend on at what age she has her first child, and how long she stays out of paid work. Having the child at age t_1 and staying out of paid work until age t_2 will imply a direct wage loss of the rectangular t_1aet_2 and a loss of returns to human capital investments forgone of abcde. Having the child at age t_2 and staying out of paid work until age t_3 will imply a direct wage loss of the area of t_2bgt_3 and a loss of returns to human capital investments forgone of bcgf.

The purpose of this chapter is to empirically estimate and compare the size of these areas. The problem can be stated as choosing the point of time (the age) to minimize the sum of direct wage forgone which we will label A and the returns to human capital investments forgone which we will label B. The direct wage cost of having the child at age i, labelled A_i is estimated by:

$$(1) \quad A_i = \frac{1}{(1+r)^{(i-i_0)}} * h * w_i$$

where index i denotes the woman's age at giving birth to her first child, h is the number of years of home time and w_i is the natural logarithm of the wage read off the wage curve of potential wages at time i. After h periods the woman is assumed, when she returns to the labour market, to be able to receive the same wage as she earned right before giving birth. Thus A_i corresponds to the rectangular areas A_1, A_2 etc. as drawn in Figure 7.1. In order to compare home time periods later in life to home time periods earlier in life we calculate the present value of the direct wage cost at i_0, the age at birth of the first child which we consider to be an early birth by discounting by the interest rate r.

The second part of the life time earnings costs is the loss of returns to human capital investments forgone B_i represented by the shaded area between the potential age earnings curve and the realised age earnings curve after having a child.

B_i is approximated by:

$$(2)\ B_i = \sum_{t=i+h}^{D} \frac{1}{(1+r)} * (w_t - w_t')$$

where w_t is the potential wage at time t and w_t' the realised wage.

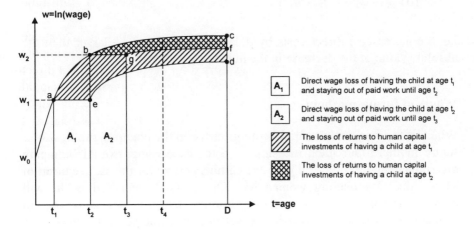

Figure 7.1: Career Costs of the Timing of First Birth

We assume that increases in earnings capacity or on the job investments can only be realized during time periods at work, but there is no net depreciation of human capital during home time periods. This means that $w^1_{i+h} = w_i$ as depicted in Figure 7.1.

Total costs of having a child at age i equals:

(3) $C_i = A_i + B_i$

where A_i increases for later births and B_i decreases for later births. If the increase in A_i exceeds the decrease in B_i it would pay to have an earlier birth otherwise it pays to delay births.

Let us consider two different time points to have a birth i and j where j is later than i. In order for the costs to increase or $\Delta C>0$ we have:

(4) $A_j + B_j - \left| A_i + B_i \right| > 0$

However we know by assumption that :

(5) $B_j - B_i < 0$

since working life is finite there will be fewer periods of loss of return to human capital investments remaining for a later birth.

Given (5) the only way for (4) to hold is that:

(6) $A_j - A_i > \left| B_j - B_i \right|$

i.e. the increase in direct costs by delaying births must be larger than the absolute value of the decrease in the human capital costs.

Wages of future mothers

Which is the relevant potential earnings curve in the planning problem of a future mother? Our ideal measure of potential earnings would be a non discriminatory full time full year age earnings curve for the same education as our decision making woman has. One possible standard is the age earnings curve of women without children, because this might be an estimate of a woman's career in the absence of caring tasks. However, the sub sample of women without children in a cross section is heterogeneous. It consists of relatively young women who start their career and later possibly will have children, and women who possibly made a splendid career because they chose not to have children. The OSA data include women 18-65 but the mean age of the subsample of working women aged

18-65 who do not have children in 1996 is 28.8. This means that most of the childless women are young and may become future mothers.

On the other hand, the sample of employed mothers consists mainly of women who returned to the labour market after being a full-time mother at home for several years. The mean age of the sample of working mothers aged 18-65 is 42.0. In The Netherlands being in paid work is a recent phenomenon for mothers with pre school children.[58]

We believe that current and prospective caring tasks are the main explanatory factor in the male/female wage gap[59] although it is well-known that the labour market is segregated according to gender. Furthermore, wage discrimination still exists between men and women often in that female dominated jobs are lower paid. Bakker, Tijdens and Winkels (1997) study the Dutch gender wage gap on a representative sample of the Dutch population (Socio Economic Panel (SEP)) from Statistics Netherlands of which they use the 1993 wave selecting employees working at least 12 hours a week. Their analysis includes variables on educational field in addition to the number of years of education, age, experience and tenure, occupational level and percentage of women in occupation. This latter variable is strongly significant and contributes 14.1 percentage points to the total male female wage gap of 36.3%.

We think that a young female economist for example will believe that her wage potential is that of economists in general. We do not believe that she discounts her career prospects because of possible sex discrimination. In The Netherlands there simply does not exist a female economists age earnings curve because until now there are few older

---

[58] Among mothers who return to work after giving birth to their first child 22% leave the labour market again after a short period, probably because they cannot make good arrangements to combine work and family. This estimate is done by Groot & Maassen van den Brink (1997) on the basis of data collected for women who had their first birth in 1991 or 1992.

[59] We assume here that men do not have current and prospective caring tasks, or do have caring tasks to a substantially lesser extent. One study (OSA, 1997) showed that this assumption is not unrealistic. Only recently some husbands started to share caring for children with their wifes, but still not more than 30% of the total number of hours that husband and wife care for their own children in households with children of age 6 or younger. The number of hours that husbands care for the home varies from 20% to 25% of the total hours that the husband and the wife spend in care for the home, in households with young children. Husbands in households with older children care to a far lesser extent. Very few persons care for other dependent people due to sickness, handicap or old age. From these caring persons 63% is female.

women who are economists.[60] We therefore believe that the relevant potential earnings against which the woman will judge her career prospects is the age earnings curve on average of narrowly defined educational groups. Therefore men's age earnings curves will be used as potential earnings for a woman in her planning decision for the timing of maternity. For data reasons however we work with three educational groups, although more detailed educational groups would have been preferred.

In Figure 7.2 log wages of men for three educational groups high education, medium education and low education are plotted against age, and quadratic age earnings curves are fitted, based on the 1996 cross section of the OSA data. We use net wages for comparison with the fertility and work history data which includes only net wages different from the 1996 cross section which includes also before tax wages. In Figure 7.3 wages of women one survey before giving birth per educational group are plotted against age and linear regressions in age are fitted. Figure 7.4 compares the fitted lines per educational group for the prebirth wages of mothers to those of men. The conclusion is that the prebirth wages are rather similar to those of men. We consider this as a justification for using age earnings curves of men as potential wages for future mothers.

A second assumption of our estimation below is that the wage that a woman receives by return to work after a period of home time is the same as that which she earned before leaving her job for childbearing and infant care. In Table 7.1 we present women's wage regressions for wages reported one survey before birth of first child and one survey after the birth of the first child. Wage before birth is determined by human capital variables age and education as expected and also wage after birth performs as expected. We have deliberately chosen for a wage regression linear in age because the fact that we only observe the lower age brackets where no levelling off of the investment profile has as yet occurred. The last column of Table 7.1 shows wage after birth as determined by wage before birth and human capital variables. The result is that only wage before remains significant. This is a justification for our assumption that upon return to work the woman's earnings capacity is about the same as it was when she left her job before giving birth.

---

[60]   In this way we ignore, of course, that   there are also many female dominated professions, for which there does not exist a males' earnings curve.

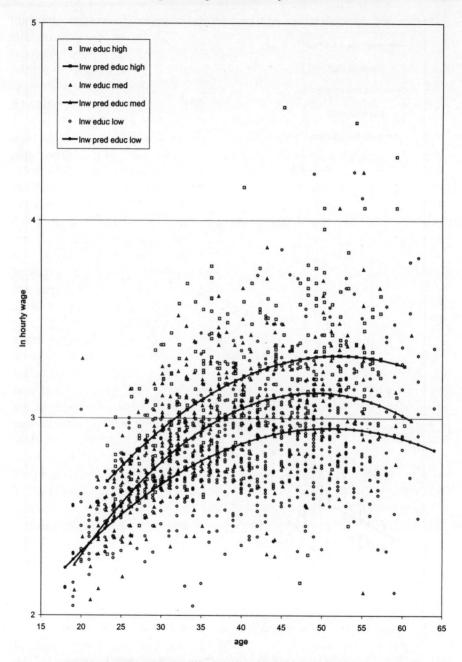

Figure 7.2: Potential Age Earnings Curves (net wages)

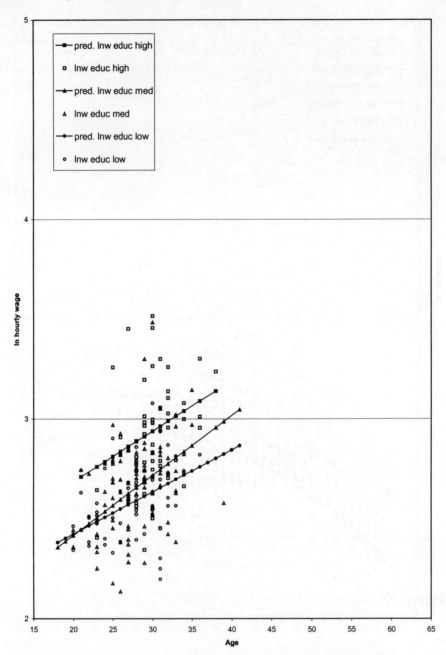

Figure 7.3: Women's Age Earnings Curves Pre-childbearing

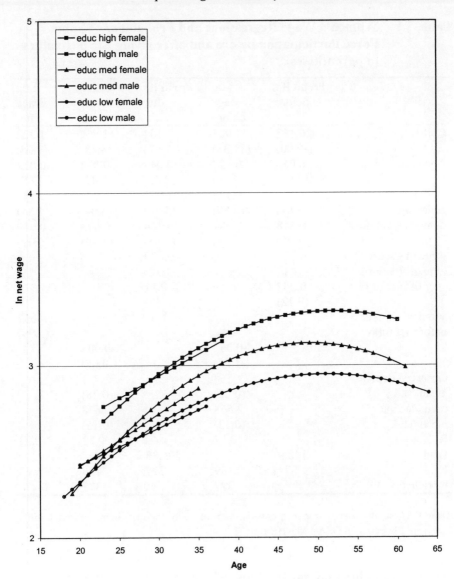

Figure 7.4: Women's Potential and Observed Age Earnings Curves

Table 7.1   Women's Wage Regressions and Probability of Labour Force Participation before and after giving Birth (t-values in parentheses)

	Probit lfp before	Log wage before	Probit lfp after	Log wage after	Log wage after
Const	-20.152	1.905	-12.104	1.969	1.372
	(-9.90)	(11.35)	(-7.63)	(8.48)	(3.58)
Age at first birth	0.066	0.023	0.049	0.024	-0.012
	(3.01)	(4.26)	(2.42)	(3.41)	(-1.49)
Dumed1,	1.054	0.138	1.022	0.274	0.154
educ=high	(3.64)	(2.89)	(4.20)	(4.04)	(1.85)
dumed2 educ=low	0.358	0.094	0.254	0.073	0.019
	(1.98)	(2.55)	(1.63)	(1.42)	(0.32)
wage of spouse at	-0.037		-0.020		
time of first birth	(-1.70)		(-1.18)		
year of first birth	0.207		0.11		
	(9.12)		(6.43)		
Women's wage					0.657
before 1st birth					(3.99)
λ		-0.067		-0.003	
		(-1.53)		(-0.05)	
Observed dep.var		2.568		2.761	
mean (st.d.)		(0.22)		(0.28)	
pred. dep.var		2.568		2.678	
mean (st.d.)		(0.12)		(0.15)	
R^2		0.37		0.32	0.31
LogL	-148.9		-205.35		
N	377	139	377	138	83
n predicted		377		377	

Data: OSA supply survey: for men cross section of 1996, for first-time mothers, fertility and work file based on OSA 1985-1996.

Simulations of life time earnings loss of timing of maternity

In this section the career costs of giving birth are simulated using expressions (1) and (2) above. In the simulations we choose i=age at giving first birth to be equal to alternatively age 23, 27, 31 and 35. Potential wage at time t is taken from the fitted quadratic age earnings curves by education for men represented in figures 7.2 and 7.4 above.[61] We also vary number of years of home time in connection with childbirth h in expressions (1) and (2) above to be either 1, 4 or 10 years. Further we use information on probability of labour force participation one survey after first birth for women who gave birth to their first child in the period 1990-1996 by educational group and information on hours of work for women who were employed one survey after giving birth to their first child. In this way the estimates of costs are changed into:

$$(7) \quad C_i = \sum_{t=i}^{i+k} \frac{1}{(1+r)^{t-i_0}} * w_i * p_e * \delta_e + \sum_{i}^{D} \frac{1}{(1+r)^{i-i_0}} (w_i - w_i^1) * p_e * \delta_e$$

$$(k = 0,1,2,...,h)$$

Period h will be called the maternity period and periods from i+h to D will be called the post maternity period. In (7) p_e = probability of being employed one survey after giving birth for the e-th educational group, e=high, medium and low and δ_e = hours of work as a fraction of full-time work for the eth educational group, e=high, medium and low. We vary these parameters to be either unity or observed during the maternity period and either unity or observed during the post maternity period.[62] Further we choose 0.02 as the discount rate.

In Table 7.2 the life time earnings loss is expressed as a fraction of potential life time earnings discounted back to age 23. It is evident from the figures that life time earnings loss decreases by postponement of maternity. The less the home time the less the life time earnings loss of course.

---

[61] The fitted age earnings curves are respectively
for high education:

$\ln w_t =$	1.253 +	0.0787t	$-0.00077t^2$
	(2.89)	(3.61)	(-2.97)

for medium education:

$\ln w_t =$	0.803 +	0.0945t	$-0.00097t^2$
	(3.79)	(8.26)	(-6.56)

for low education:

$\ln w_t =$	1.258 +	0.0663t	$-0.00065t^2$
	(9.12)	(9.26)	(-7.35)

[62] P_e observed two surveys after birth is for e=high 0.86, for e=medium 0.59 and for e=low 0.32. Hours of work per week varied for e=high 22 hours, e=medium 21 hours and e=low 18 hours. In the simulations hours of work are divided by 38 which currently is the standard full time hours of work in The Netherlands.

The life time earnings losses under simulation 1.1. where only time out varies by number of years are similar over the educational groups. However if you plan to be a full time home maker during 10 years the loss will be about 24% of potential life time earnings if you have your child at age 35 in comparison to having a child at 23 which means a loss of 31% of potential life time earnings. If part time work becomes a life long behaviour in the post maternity period as in simulation 1.2 the earnings loss will be 30 to 50% of potential earnings for all educational groups. Since hours of work of employed women in the early 1990s post maternity period do not differ very much between educational groups we also have little variation in earnings loss. In the simulations 2.1 earnings of the post maternity period varies by observed employment probabilities, where there are big differences between educational groups. The variation in life time earnings loss is then large between educational groups. Whereas high educated women lose at a maximum 40.5% of potential life time earnings the loss always amounts to more than 45% for low educated women with a maximum of 77.1% for a low educated woman who decides to have a child at age 23 stay out for 10 years full time and then have the observed probability of becoming employed afterwards.

In the simulations 2.2. we assume that in the maternity period the woman is full time home maker but in the post maternity period she has a probability of being employed which is the same as what we observe one survey after giving birth for mothers who gave birth to their first child in 1990-1996. Likewise hours of work of employed women are assumed to be equal to observed. In simulations 2.2 we therefore assume that the probability of employment and hours of work of employed women will remain the same for the whole post maternity period until retirement. With these assumptions life time earnings loss will vary across educational groups with low educated women losing at least 56% of potential life time earnings and at most 88.5% and high educated women losing a minimum of 33.7 per cent and a maximum of 65.1%. Losses of this magnitude have been the rule for Dutch women of earlier cohorts. Dankmeijer (1996) on the basis of the cross section of 1990 and with earnings of women without children as potential earnings finds that women lose 90% of potential life time earnings, that middle educated lose 30% and that high educated lose 14% respectively. Mertens (1998) uses a cross section of 1992 to simulate life time earnings also with women without children as the potential earnings standard. Mertens (1998 p.183) estimates the loss of potential life time earnings to be 62% for a medium educated woman who has an early birth and 44% if she has a later birth.

In the simulations (3) we relax the assumption that the maternity period (h) is devoted full time to unpaid work at home and assume that the probability of being employed equals the observed for recent mothers only in the maternity period but in the post maternity period all the women are employed. In the simulations 3.1 they also all work full time in the post maternity period whereas in 3.2 they work part time for the rest of their lives.

Dutch public policies for parents to combine work and family can rather be characterised as assuming that full time home time during maternity is never even so long as one year. Simulations (4) take account of this option setting h=0. In principle policies allow parents to work part time unpaid as long as they themselves find appropriate. In all the simulations where part time work continues for the whole post maternity period the loss of potential life time earnings is substantial and the loss is always smaller the later the woman enters into maternity.

Life time earnings gain by postponement of first birth

In Table 7.3 we present cumulative frequencies of first births over age of the mother for the 1980s and 1990s separately. Postponement of birth is clearly visible for all three educational groups. Also more educated women have their children later than less educated women. In the 1980s by age 23 only 4% of high educated women, 22% of medium educated women and 31 per cent of low educated women had given birth to their first child. Women with medium or low education have postponed their first child's birth beyond age 27 to a very large extent comparing the 1980s to the 1990s. Whereas 70% of these women had their first child by age 27 in the 1980s the percentage had decreased to 45% for women with medium education and to 54% for women with low education.

Table 7.2: Present Value of Lifetime Earnings Loss as a Fraction of Potential Lifetime Earnings by Education, of having the First Child at Different Ages (23,27,31,35)

Education	high 23	high 27	high 31	high 35	medium 23	medium 27	medium 31	medium 35	low 23	low 27	low 31	low 35
Age at maternity: i												
1. Maternity=h, $p_e=\delta_e=0$												
1.1 Post Maternity=D-h-i, $p_e=\delta_e=1$												
H=1	0.035	0.032	0.030	0.028	0.034	0.032	0.029	0.027	0.034	0.032	0.030	0.028
H=4	0.134	0.124	0.115	0.107	0.132	0.123	0.113	0.105	0.133	0.123	0.114	0.106
H=10	0.310	0.286	0.263	0.242	0.309	0.284	0.261	0.238	0.307	0.283	0.261	0.239
1.2 Post M=D-h-i, $p_e=1$ δ_e=observed												
H=1	0.441	0.390	0.341	0.287	0.467	0.413	0.361	0.310	0.543	0.479	0.417	0.360
H=4	0.498	0.440	0.390	0.338	0.520	0.463	0.406	0.352	0.589	0.522	0.456	0.393
H=10	0.596	0.531	0.470	0.410	0.649	0.548	0.482	0.419	0.666	0.591	0.518	0.449
2. Maternity=h, $p_e=\delta_e=0$												
2.1 Post M=D-h-i, p_e=observed $\delta_e=1$												
H=1	0.169	0.151	0.133	0.134	0.430	0.381	0.333	0.286	0.691	0.610	0.530	0.454
h=4	0.255	0.230	0.207	0.184	0.488	0.435	0.382	0.331	0.722	0.718	0.556	0.478
h=10	0.405	0.368	0.332	0.298	0.590	0.523	0.463	0.404	0.771	0.680	0.594	0.510
2.2 Post M=D-h-i, $p_e=\delta_e$=observed												
h=1	0.520	0.459	0.401	0.337	0.685	0.606	0.528	0.453	0.853	0.753	0.654	0.560
h=4	0.568	0.505	0.442	0.383	0.717	0.635	0.555	0.476	0.868	0.765	0.666	0.570
h=10	0.651	0.579	0.510	0.443	0.770	0.681	0.594	0.510	0.885	0.779	0.676	0.578

3. Maternity=h, p_e=observed, δ_e=1											
3.1 Post M=D-h-i, $p_e=\delta_e=1$											
h=4	0.033	0.027	0.022	0.018	0.064	0.056	0.049	0.044	0.096	0.088	0.080	0.074
h=10	0.073	0.059	0.049	0.040	0.147	0.130	0.116	0.104	0.225	0.207	0.191	0.179
3.2 Post M=D-h-i, $p_e=1$ δ_e=observed											
h=4	0.398	0.346	0.296	0.249	0.452	0.396	0.342	0.290	0.552	0.486	0.423	0.362
h=10	0.359	0.305	0.255	0.209	0.453	0.394	0.337	0.284	0.584	0.515	0.448	0.389
4. Maternity h=0											
4.1 Post M=D-h-i, p_e=observed δ_e=1	0.140	0.124	0.108	0.092	0.410	0.362	0.316	0.270	0.680	0.599	0.521	0.446
4.2 Post M=D-h-i, $p_e=\delta_e$=observed	0.502	0.443	0.386	0.331	0.674	0.596	0.519	0.444	0.840	0.744	0.643	0.550
4.3 Post M=D-h-i, $p_e=1$ δ_e= observed	0.421	0.372	0.324	0.277	0.447	0.389	0.344	0.295	0.526	0.463	0.403	0.345
4.4 Post M=D-h-i, $p_e=1$ $\delta_e=0.5$	0.500	0.441	0.384	0.329	0.500	0.442	0.385	0.329	0.500	0.442	0.385	0.329
4.5 Post M=D-h-i, p_e=observ. $\delta_e=0.5$	0.570	0.503	0.438	0.375	0.705	0.623	0.543	0.464	0.848	0.748	0.650	0.556

Data:OSA.90-96; h=maternity period in years of home time, p_e is probability of labour force participation for educational group e=high, middle and low. δ_e=hours of market work as a fraction of full time work for educational group e, D= age at retirement, i=age at giving birth. Discount rate is 0.02. Women's observed participation rate and hours per week one survey after giving birth to their first child, for women who gave birth to their first child during 1990-1996. Employment probability upon return are for high education 0.86, for medium education 0.59 and for low education 0.32. Hours of Work observed by return are for high education 22, for medium education 21 and for low education 18 hours per week.

Table 7.3: Cumulative Proportion of Mothers According to Age at First Birth, Education and Time Period

	High	Med	Low	High	Med	Low	All	All
Age- (yrs)	80-89	80-89	80-89	90-96	90-96	90-96	80-89	90-96
21	1.89	6.71	15.49	2.78	1.00	8.11	10.51	3.74
23	3.77	22.15	30.99	5.56	6.00	25.68	24.53	13.08
25	11.32	46.98	50.00	8.33	21.00	44.59	43.94	27.57
27	22.64	69.13	71.13	22.22	46.00	54.05	64.15	44.86
29	56.60	85.23	80.99	41.67	70.00	75.68	79.51	66.82
31	83.02	92.62	92.96	69.44	83.00	85.14	90.84	81.31
33	92.54	97.99	96.48	83.33	95.00	93.24	96.50	92.06
35	98.11	99.33	97.89	86.11	97.00	98.65	98.65	95.33
37	100.00	100.00	99.30	97.22	99.00	99.57	99.73	98.13
39	100.00	100.00	100.00	100.00	100.00	100.00	100.00	99.53
41	100.00	100.00	100.00	100.00	100.00	100.00	100.00	100.00
n	53	149	142	36	100	74	371	214
mean	29.08	26.09	25.58	30.08	28.24	26.81	26.24	28.06
(st.d.)	(2.83)	(3.43)	(4.16)	(3.73)	(3.52)	(4.01)	(3.88)	(3.92)

Own calculations based on OSA 1985-1996. Education: high: university or higher vocational training; medium: high school or middle vocational training; low: compulsory education or more but less than high school. 80-89 means that births occurred in the period 1980-1989; 90-96 means that the birth occurred in the period 1990-1996.

The distribution of first births to high educated women is pushed further into older first time mothers. In the 1980s by age 31 as many as 83 per cent had become mothers but in the 1990s this same proportion was reached not before age 33. As many as 14% of the first time mothers with high education had their first birth after age 35. The postponement of motherhood across educational groups is presented in the last two columns of Table 7.3. Whereas in the 1980s by age 31 there remained 9% of first births yet to come this was the case for 19% of first births in the 1990s.

Looking at the lifetime earnings loss computed in Table 7.2 above women have been rational in delaying first birth. Consider women of medium length education who perform according to the incentives given by Dutch combination of work and family strategy policies of the 1990s. According to Dutch policies maternity leave is 16 weeks of which 6-8 weeks have to be taken before giving birth. Therefore the mother returns to work when the child is 10 weeks old. In our simulations of Table 7.2 this corresponds to h=0 because she is not staying full time at home for one year. She does not have job protection for more than 16 weeks different from Germany and Sweden. However she has the right to keep her job and work at least 50% of full time and this is also what Dutch mothers of the 1990s do if they are employed, the average hours of work per week being 21 for medium educated women as observed one survey after first birth. The Netherlands is the most part time working country among all countries we have statistics for i.e. certainly among all OECD countries. The most relevant entry of Table 7.2 therefore probably is simulation 4.2. If the pattern of mother's age at first child birth of the 1980s had continued 17 per cent more women would have given birth by age 23. Now instead they postpone first birth say to age 27 and therefore lose 44.3% of potential life time earnings instead of 50.2%. Another 23% according to Table 7.3 would have given birth by age 27 if the age pattern of birthgiving had remained the same in the 1990s as it was in the 1980s. This means that their life time earnings loss is reduced to 38.6% of potential life time earnings. There are therefore substantial gains to be made by postponement of birth. These costs are of course also costs to the whole Dutch society because the market earnings forgone would otherwise have increased the Gross Domestic Product in The Netherlands and thus increased income per capita.

However it may be the case that the 1990 generation of Dutch women will reenter full time employment after an extended period of half time work. Say that our medium educated woman works 21 hours per week during four years and then returns to full time work. We then need to look at simulation 3.1 for h=4 and we can see that life time earnings loss will be limited to 4.4. to 6.4% of potential life time earnings and that the maximum gain of postponement is only 2% of potential life time earnings.

We started this chapter by giving some information about medical costs associated with postponement of births. Such costs would in principle offset the costs of life time earnings loss as would also the costs of day care which the mother otherwise would do as unpaid work at home. Costs of using biomedical techniques for conception is one aspect of such costs. Other aspects of costs are associated with health of children and health of mothers. It is known that the risk of being born with Down syndrome increases as the mother is older. We do not know if older mothers are observed to have more health risks in connection with births but if this is the case such costs should also be included.

In the Dutch 1990s subsidised day care is available only for about 7 per cent of pre-school children and market priced day care for children is expensive to families. One year full time day care for a pre school child costs Dfl 18,000.[63] Suppose a young couple needs to pay after subsidy Dfl 1,000 per month for 5 days care for their first child and their net combined income is Dfl 5,000. Given individual taxes, day care fees and the legal right to keep a job on a part time basis it will be an economically attractive option for the couple to share: mother cares for the child at home one day and works 4 days, father cares for the child at home a different day, childcare is paid for 3 days or maybe even 2 days if there is a grandmother who volunteers for one day a week, a situation that would not be unusual given the fact that within the generation of women with adult children more than 50% are housewives (OSA, Kunnen et al.1997). Results of Sundström and Rönsen (1996) comparing family policies of Sweden and Norway over time show that the longer the job protection period the sooner recent mothers return to work because more mothers can arrange satisfactory day care for a one year old or 18 months year old child than for a two months old child. This implies that more Dutch mothers would probably keep their jobs after maternity, which is a factor that decreases life time earnings loss and therefore decreases the gains of postponement of maternity. Whereas there is an economic rational for working part time during periods when day care costs are paid the economics of continuing to work part time when such costs are not anymore paid are different. However, if as the goal is for Dutch equal opportunity policies, a shorter work week will apply in equal amount for men and women this is a life quality gain for the society.

---

[63]   Care during irregular hours (in the evening, during weekends or holidays) costs about 25% more. Day care for the second child costs for parents about one third of the price for the care of the first child. After school care for one child 5 days costs about Dfl 350 for parents with a net income of at least Dfl 5,000. Again these there is a discount price for the second child's care. Some schools have opening hours till 2 in the afternoon, which means that children of age 4-12 need after school care every day.

Conclusions

Postponement of maternity in The Netherlands is becoming a political and medical concern. We showed in this chapter that it will always result in a life time earnings gain to have first birth later in life. The life time earnings loss consists of parts; first the wage loss during what we call the maternity period and second the lower earnings of the postmaternity period. The lower earnings of the postmaternity period consist of two components first the wage loss caused by investments in human capital forgone during home time and second the smaller labour supply of mothers as compared to individuals without caring tasks.

The smaller labour supply in turn is composed of smaller probability of labour force participation and the large likelihood of working part time among mothers. The total life time earnings loss always decreases for later births in comparison to earlier births. Given observed probability of labour force participation and hours of work by women who gave birth to their first child women with higher education are likely to realise a smaller loss in lifetime earnings than women of medium or low education. Women of higher education are also the ones who postpone birth of first child the most but the increase in age at maternity from births in the 1980s to births in the 1990s is considerable for all educational groups. For example whereas 80% of all births in the 1980s occurred by age 29 of the women this was only true for 66% in the 1990s. At age 25 in the 1980s 44% of first births had occurred but in the 1990s this was only true for 26%. The increasing age at maternity is accompanied by larger contributions of women to the gross domestic product and therefore increasing per capita incomes which exceed the costs of day-care for children which this scenario necessitates because the production consequences are for the entire lifetime of the woman. However this increase in age at maternity is also accompanied by larger biomedical costs as documented in the introduction to this chapter. Further possible health consequences to mothers and children have not been considered in this study and these perspectives call for interdisciplinary work including medicine and economics.

8 Summary

Chapter 1 addresses why and how this book analyses women's labour market position in Germany, Great Britain, The Netherlands and Sweden in the period they plan and actually have children. Women in these countries have increased their educational level and their labour force participation rates during the 1980s and 1990s. For increasing numbers of young couples the question of how to fit a birth into a woman's curriculum vitae is a difficult decision problem. In this book we are mainly interested in women's human capital accumulation before they give birth and in the immediate period after giving birth. Labour force participation, hours of work and wages in the period around child birth are considered to be crucial for the women's later life time career. Also characteristics of the spouse such as earnings have an influence on the decision when to fit a birth into the woman's curriculum vitae. Social costs of incompatibility of paid work and children include for example depreciation of women's human capital investment, women's loss of economic independence, possible harm to children if parents have less time for their children, medical costs related to having children beyond the optimal biological age. Governments in different countries have developed social policies on the combination of work and children. There are differences in expenditure and in ideology of family values and economic independence of household members.

In Chapter 2 the governmental policies on the family of Germany, Great Britain, The Netherlands and Sweden are characterised making use of Esping-andersen's (1990) welfare state typology and Sainsbury's (1994) gender based welfare state typology. These policies have been used to formulate hypotheses on women's labour force behaviour in connection with childbirth laid out in Chapters 4-7. Chapter 3 describes and comments on the choice and construction of variables from household panel data sets collected in the countries included. A comparative fertility and work file has been created including monthly changes in women's labour market position in the period of birth giving. Chapter 4 empirically investigates labour force transitions in connection with child birth by birth order in

Germany, Great Britain, Sweden and The Netherlands. Furthermore the determinants of being a career oriented mother are analysed considering the labour force status three months before giving birth and twenty four months after giving birth. In addition the determinants of the likelihood of entering the labour market rather quickly after giving birth are empirically analysed. In Chapter 5 we analyse the short term effect of childbearing on women's career and earnings for first and second births in Germany and Sweden. The hypothesis is that human capital accumulated before first birth will determine earnings during and after mothering. The determinants of the share of women's earnings in combined market earnings of the household after child birth is decomposed into predicted wage, probability of labour force participation and predicted hours of work given labour market participation. In Chapters 6 and 7 we empirically analyse to what extent economic factors are responsible for the decisions on delaying the time of first birth. Chapter 6 explains how decisions on the timing of births are influenced by economic factors such as opportunity costs of time, which primarily consist of labour market income forgone and investments in human capital forgone. Chapter 7 estimates the gains in life time earnings by education that women have made by postponement of maternity in The Netherlands analysing potential earnings curves and women's wages, labour force participation and hours of work after giving birth.

Breadwinner ideology against individual and equal role sharing ideology

Women will choose to remain working at home or to enter market work depending on the net benefits in a broad sense from choosing one of the alternatives. A number of factors influence this choice and have been discussed in chapter 2. These factors are, the tax and benefit system (Blundell 1993; B. Gustafsson and Klevmarken 1993; Zimmermann 1993), whether taxes are jointly or individually assessed (Gustafsson 1992; Gustafsson and Bruyn-Hundt 1991; Nelson 1991), day care subsidies, availability of good quality child care (Gustafsson and Stafford 1992; Leibowitz et al. 1992), the duration and replacement ratio of parental or maternity leaves (Sundström and Stafford 1992), the organisation of the school day and after school care, the availability of (part-time) jobs and finally regulation as regards leave for caring for sick children. In all these respects, Sweden has chosen a policy mix that benefits the two-earner family according to an ideology of individual responsibility and equal role sharing which began in the 1930s and 1940s inspired by the 1934 book by Alva and Gunnar Myrdal on the Population Crisis (Gustafsson 1994).

Germany on the other hand, has chosen policies that benefit the one earner family according to the breadwinner ideology (Sainsbury (ed) 1994; Gustafsson 1984, 1994; Gustafsson and Stafford 1994, 1995)offering tax-benefits to one earner/one carer couples, long maternity leave period with low pay, part-time child care facilities and part-time school day. The Netherlands changed from mostly bread winner oriented social policies in the 1960s and 1970s to mostly equal role sharing social policies in the 1990s. On the breadwinner-individual model axis the United Kingdom takes a place in between the breadwinner and the individual model of governmental policies on the family.

The type of welfare state ideology also influences policy choice. Germany is the prototype of the conservative corporatist welfare state. Also The Netherlands till the 1990s to a large extent falls into this category. Sweden is the prototype of the institutional universal social democrat welfare state. A third type of welfare state is characterised as the liberal or residual welfare state with the United States as the prototype. Great Britain as regards policies for the family to a large extent fall into this category. In comparison to Germany, The Netherlands and Sweden very little government support to families with children exists and having children is seen as a private concern. Individual parents can enjoy better provisions than the national standards if they work with an employer who has as a result of negotiations conceded to better provisions. Since the 1990s the Dutch government stimulates employers to create child care facilities for employees, subsidies for child care capacity have been increased and employees' right to work part time and the right to increase work hours again are on the political agenda. However, only the collective labour agreements for government employees allow half a year paid parental leave as compared to national legislation which allows only unpaid leave.

Making use of the 'fertility and work' files which we created out of the national household panel data sets as described in Chapter 3, the purpose of Chapter 4 has been to analyse labour force transitions around childbirth and the extent to which these lower labour force participation rates of mothers are explained by policies in connection with childbirth.

Labour market status before entering motherhood

Twelve months before birth should indicate the situation before any adjustments in connection with birth have been made and three months before birth could possibly be the beginning of adjustments. Although the proportion participating in the labour market of first time mothers 12 months before giving birth to the first child is highest in Sweden, the proportion of these being in full-time work is lower than in Germany and Great Britain. In this respect Sweden does not appear to be the work society it is usually considered to be and which is also the intention of the institutional welfare state.

Among German women both in West and East Germany, two thirds are in full-time work three months before the birth of the first child as against only 51.1% of the Swedish women. This result may imply that German women make the most of their working life before becoming mothers because they know they will soon enter into the status of home maker.

Of the groups considered in Table 4.1 only immigrant women in West Germany are full-time home makers to any large extent before they have children. In this group 27% are full time home makers 12 months before the first child is born and 41% 3 months before the first child is born. There is a considerable decrease in probability of full-time work from 12 months before having the first child to 3 months before giving birth among immigrant women in Germany. In West Germany part-time work does not increase during this period, but in East Germany it does. Being on maternity leave does increase as the date of birth is approaching, and in Sweden this increase is relatively large. A rational Swedish mother to be should make sure her income is as large as possible right before birth. The drop in 'long part-time' and increase in 'on leave' between 3 and 12 months confirms such behaviour, but the low full-time participation rate does not.

In East Germany the drop from 83% full-time a year before birth of the first child to 66% three months before birth is accompanied by an increase in total unemployment and an increase in part-time work. This may be a period phenomenon caused by reunification which resulted in an increase in unemployment in the new German states of former East Germany from 10% in 1991 to 21% in 1993. Similarly, the decrease of full-time and the increase of part-time work may be explained, by demand for labour considerations particular in this period rather than labour supply considerations of wishing to size down work efforts before birth. In West Germany the drop in full-time work is accommodated by increases in unemployment and unpaid work at home both among German women and immigrant women.

The lowest employment rate 3 months before first birth is found among women in Great Britain (51%) and Immigrants in West Germany

(43%). According to Table 4.1, the employment rate of British first-time mothers declines sharply between 12 and 3 months before birth from 79% to 51%. A large proportion of British women end up in leave of absence three months before birth but unlike mothers in Sweden and similar to immigrant women in Germany the largest proportion of British women end up in unpaid work at home three months before birth. The most likely explanation is that during the observation period a high proportion of the economically active British women were not entitled to maternity leave.

Because Swedish women lose benefits during parental leave if they have smaller earnings three months before birth, we had expected Swedish women to be more work-oriented right before birth than women of the other countries where benefits are unrelated to previous earnings. However this is not what we find. The tight labour market in Sweden until 1991 may have induced women into thinking that the risk of losing their job was small so that they chose to be on leave rather than to be at work.

Flows into and out of the labour force 3 months before and 24 months after child birth

Section 4.5 examined the group of women with certain characteristics that are career-oriented in the sense that they were participating in the labour force until 3 months before birth of their child and returned to wage employment after the end of legal maternity leave, which we chose to be 24 months after the birth of the child. The choice of 24 months was to capture career-oriented women under the German provisions, which allowed for 24 months job protection until 1992, whereas the Swedish job protection period is 18 months. For Great Britain, and The Netherlands this time span after childbirth may not be as useful at capturing career oriented women, because the job security period is only 6.7 months in Britain and 6 months per parent in The Netherlands since 1990 but only paid in public sector.

In each successive birth order among West German and Dutch women, the group of continuous labour force participants (ee) decreases while the group of continuous home makers (hh) increases to well over half of the women. Among Swedish women the group of continuous career women remains about half of all women who had their child during the observation period, also for the higher birth orders while the group of continuous home makers remains a minority of about 12% of all women having a child. The employment rate declines to 57.8 after the birth of the first child. The proportion of women in 'eh' is higher after the first birth, whereas the proportion 'he' is higher after the second birth. This is consistent with findings of Hoem (1993) and indicates that Swedish women are making use of the "speed premium", which means that maternity pay will be based on earnings before the first birth if the second child is born within 30 months after the first child.

The British low employment rates before and after birth are also reflected in the small proportion of 'ee' mothers in Great Britain. Only 23% of the British first-time mothers were employed three months before and 24 months after first birth. The findings of other British studies suggest that our proportion of 'ee' mothers is low (Macran et al. 1995) and that more mothers do return if we would have chosen an earlier month, for example 12 months instead of 24 months after childbearing. Because of the poorer maternity leave provisions, many British women return to work earlier. The short supply of day care and the costs of care will also contribute to some mothers either not returning to work after childbirth, or not continuing to work for much longer after they have returned. Also the transferable ZRA (see chapter 2) creates disincentives for secondary earners, mostly women to work. The proportion of recent mothers in Great Britain who are not employed 24 months after the second and third birth is much higher than in Sweden.

Determinants of being a career oriented mother

The next step is to analyse the probability of being an 'ee' woman when considering women's own human capital and the income of her spouse. For German women in West Germany and for Dutch women the results tell a convincing story that the human capital accumulated by the women before the birth of the child matters in determining whether or not she is an 'ee' woman. The longer the education of the woman and the more labour market experience she had before birth the more likely she is to have a continuous labour force career. This is true irrespective of birth order. The breadwinner ideology would assume that wives of richer husbands do not have to work in the market so that we could expect a negative influence from husband's income on the probability of being an 'ee' woman. Only for second births of West German women we see that the husband's income is significant. A higher income then increases rather than decreases the likelihood of the mother being a continuous labour force participant. This suggests assortative mating in the marriage market rather than a breadwinner effect. For The Netherlands we do not find that husband's income is significant. Further we expected that women whose husbands relative to themselves had larger human capital would be less likely to be career women. In a more extended logit model we measured this by the difference in years of schooling but this variable was never significant, nor was the age differential significant. Finally it may be expected that women who do not intend to have another child may have a different labour force behaviour than women who expect to have another child in the near future. We entered a dummy variable for not having another child during observation period, but the variable was not significant. The findings on the determinants of being an 'ee' woman among immigrant women in Germany are similar to those for West German women; the woman's own human capital determines her behaviour while husband's income does not influence the woman's choice for a continuous career.

Joshi et al. (1995) suggest that polarisation has been occurring between low and highly educated women. Highly educated women who delayed their first birth, built up work experience before birth and were able to use the new maternity legislation and pay for child care. In their analysis, the age of the mother at child birth became insignificant when education and work experience were included since those who delay return are less educated and had their child at an early age. Similar findings are obtained in studies by Dale and Joshi (1992), Jenkins (1994), Gregg and Wadsworth (1995). Our results in Table 4.3 do not reflect such polarisation, rather we find that the woman's own human capital i.e. education and labour force experience determine whether or not she is in market work both three months before and twenty four months after birth.

Turning to a similar analysis for Sweden we get much less precise and insignificant results. We are inclined to believe that these results reflect real differences in comparison to the other countries. Swedish mothers are able to combine work and family also with fairly small amounts of human capital. German and Dutch women can act according to the individual equal role sharing model only if they are well educated. If they are less educated the breadwinner ideology and institutions put them into the home maker position.

The timing of entering the labour force after birth

In section 4.6 we analyse how long it takes before recent mothers enter market work for the first time after birth. We do not require that the woman remains in the labour market for an extended period. Such a restriction on the data would lower the numbers because in all the groups studied there is a considerable amount of in and out movements. We also analyse return to the labour market regardless of having a subsequent child. The effect of subsequent children on return to work after the first child birth is included in Chapter 6.

The cumulative proportion of recent mothers still not entering the labour market by three monthly intervals after birth controlling for the exposure to risk, shows that very few mothers were at work 3 months after child birth in any of the groups we studied. Interestingly and consistent with the shorter job protection period, Dutch and British mothers entered a job considerably sooner after birth than women in Sweden and Germany. Already three months after the birth of the first child 28% of Dutch women returned to their job. It takes nine months before one quarter of British mothers are in market work after the first birth but after six months already 15% are employed. The differences between Sweden and Germany are very small when comparing the proportion of mothers who are employed when the child is 6 months old, and it does not differ between the first and second birth. When the child is twelve months old the Swedish mothers are much more likely to be in market work than the German mothers. This difference between the two countries becomes more pronounced as the child grows older. When the child is three years old 80% of Swedish mothers have entered the labour market compared to 55% of the German women and 43% of immigrant women in West Germany. When the child is three, the proportion of women observed in the labour market after birth is highest in Sweden at every birth order. But the Dutch figure is almost on the same level as the Swedish figure with only 24% have not yet re-entered the labour market.

The proportional hazard models of the duration in months before entering market work for mothers after childbirth presented in Table 4.5 show that among West German women, at the mean experience, the older the woman is at the child's birth, the later she returns. At the mean age at childbirth, the more market related human capital she accumulated before the birth of her first child, the earlier she entered employment. Income of the spouse has a significantly negative effect implying that women with richer husbands delay their entrance to the labour force. Time dummies to capture changes in the German job protection period were never significant. The only difference between immigrants and other West German women is that years of employment experience is the most important explanatory factor when analysing the tempo of entering the labour market after birth of immigrants, while educational level is most important for West Germans. This is irrespective of birth order.

The regression on the Swedish duration before entering work after second birth shows that education does not influence the timing of entering employment. After the second birth, a mother returns to work later the older she was at birth of her second child (at mean work experience). The positive interaction effect between age of the mother and her experience for second time mothers in Sweden indicates that at ages above the mean, more employment experience increases the tempo of entering the labour market after birth while the opposite is true at younger ages at second birth. We do not find any significant results for first births, which may have to do with the fact that about 80% of Swedish women who have one child proceed to have a second child and it is profitable to have the second child soon after the first without re-entering.

In contrast to the German and Swedish mothers, British mothers of 2 or 3 children are in employment sooner the older they are at childbirth. This result is consistent with other British studies which have found that career oriented women who are also highly educated, delay childbirth and return quicker after giving birth when their maternity leave has expired (Macran et al. 1995; Joshi et al. 1995). The variable that controls for interaction between age and experience turned out to be significant for the first child, revealing a positive effect of more work experience on return to work, but the effect declines with age at motherhood.

Chapter 5 concentrates on the economic vulnerability that women experience around childbirth. Whereas the long run effects of labour force interruptions on earnings have been researched both using cross sectional data (Mincer and Polacheck 1974, Corcoran & Duncan 1978, Dankmeyer 1996, Gustafsson 1981, Albrecht et al. 1997) and using longitudinal data (Mincer and ofek 1982) chapter 5 focuses on the short run effects. We use information on earnings for the women and their spouses, taking one wave before birth and two waves after birth, which is approximately two years, to compute women's contribution to family earnings before and after giving birth.

Women's contribution to family income

Swedish women go through the childbearing process with only a small drop in earnings. The variation in the proportion of family income earned by the women in Sweden varies from 44% before first birth to 34% after second birth. The smallest earnings of German women occur after the birth of the first child and before the second child when German women only secure 12 to 14% of family earned income. German women have smaller earnings in comparison to their husbands than Swedish women have. Swedish women however always lower their earnings after birth in comparison to before childbearing. This is true also for German first time mothers but not for German second time mothers who rather increase their earnings after their second birth in comparison to before their second birth.

German women who worked two years after the second birth seem to be a select group. The results indicate that husbands of these women decrease their earnings after the second birth and that the average earnings of the women exceed that of their husbands. Swedish husbands on the other hand in all three panels of Table 5.1 increase their earnings after birth of their child in comparison to before the child was born.

The increase from earnings before the birth of the child compared to earnings after the birth of the child among Swedish husbands only varies from one% to 12%. The German data show much more dramatic changes both for mothers and fathers. Fathers increase their earnings after birth of first child. For the German mothers there are dramatic decreases in income after first child and substantial increases after the second child is born. The exception is in panel C of the select group of mothers who were employed after first birth where first time mothers also increase their earnings from before to after birth of the first child.

Results of estimations on labour supply of recent mothers

Most studies of women's labour supply include variables on family composition, number of children and children's age (Killingsworth & Heckman (1986), Gustafsson (1992), Vlasblom (1998)). In this study we have instead selected the women at precisely the same moment in their family building cycle namely at the point of having their first birth or second birth respectively.

We hypothesise that human capital accumulated before birth of first child will determine earnings during and after mothering of pre-school children. The wage and income variables perform with expected results for the labour force participation decision 24 months after birth of the first child for first time German mothers. The higher her own predicted wage the more likely she is to participate in the labour force and the higher her husband's income the less likely she is to participate in the labour force. German second time mothers base their decision on hours of work and labour force participation on their predicted wage before first birth. The wage effect is positive implying that women with higher wages work longer hours i.e. the substitution effect is larger than the income effect, which agrees with other research on women's labour supply.

The results of the Swedish regressions are less conclusive than the results of the German regressions. We find that the higher the first time mother's wage, the more likely she is to participate in the labour force but she does not base the decision on hours of work on her wage. Husband's income does not have a significant effect on either a first time mother's labour supply decision or on a second time Swedish mother's labour force decision. This result is in line with results in Chapter 4 which showed that about 80% of Swedish mothers are labour force participants within 24 months after giving birth to a child.

Decomposition of after birth's earnings: a comparison between Germany and Sweden using simulations

We find that wages of German mothers who were labour force participants 24 months after birth are larger than wages of Swedish mothers but hours of work are smaller for German than for Swedish mothers so that the total difference in average monthly income of working mothers is within 200 Deutsche Marks per month i.e. 10% of a monthly income.

The proportion of wife's earnings in couples joint earnings for the subgroup of women who worked when their child was two years old, does not differ very much between Germany and Sweden. The variation is from 0.35 to 0.43. The large difference between Germany and Sweden is in labour force participation of mothers when the child is about two years old. Whereas 38% of first time mothers and 31% of second time German mothers were in paid work when their child was two years old, this was true for 77% of first time Swedish mothers and 81% of second time Swedish mothers. The average income of all German mothers including nonparticipants in the labour force is therefore less than half of that of Swedish first time mothers and less than one third of that of second time Swedish mothers. The resulting proportion of couple's earnings contributed by the wife is therefore not more than 16% for German first time mothers compared to 35% for Swedish first time mothers and 12 per cent for German second time mothers compared to 34% for Swedish second time mothers.

We use a simple model to predict the woman's contribution to family earnings. The prediction is fairly close, within a few percentage points of the observed women's contribution to family earnings, with the biggest relative discrepancy being that the prediction for German first time mothers show that they contribute 13% of earnings in panel 5.4B whereas it is 16% in panel 5.4A and 14% in Table 5.1A. However the differences between our two countries are much bigger. The overall result is that German mothers would, given their characteristics, have increased their earnings from about 11 to 16% of family earnings to 30 to 32% of family earnings if they had behaved according to Swedish regressions. Furthermore, Swedish mothers would have decreased their earnings' share in the family earnings from about 33 to 38% to about 17 to 21%. We believe that these differences can be ascribed to the fact that there are many more facilities to combine work and family in Sweden than in Germany due to better provisions in family policies as explained in Chapter 2.

Public policies and timing of birth

Chapter 6 analyses timing of first birth in Sweden, Germany and Great Britain. In Sweden we may expect fewer differences between more economically productive women and less economically productive women because of policies to combine work and family. However Swedish mothers to be have a financial incentive to postpone birth until they have earned a fairly high income because parental benefits for 12 months are based on earnings before birth, 90% for one month and 75% for 11 months. In addition the so-called 'speed premium' makes clustering of births a profitable option which should distinguish Swedish women's behaviour from behaviour in the other two countries. In Germany the combination of work and family is not facilitated by social policies, rather the contrary. The incentive for highly economically productive women to postpone births is therefore strong. Once the first child has been born, a rapid return to paid work is unlikely. German women considering spacing their children close together rather than two shorter career interruptions are not influenced by public policies and should therefore be indifferent between the two choices. Because Germany favours full-time maternal care rather than assisting mothers to combine work with family, there could be a demarcation line between the highly productive women who want to combine work and family and others who do not wish or cannot struggle against the 'male breadwinner' organisation of the German society. Individual human capital considerations will be more important in Germany than in Sweden. The same reasoning applies for British women since they are not assisted by public policies to combine work and family.

Timing of first birth

The micro data show that in all three countries more highly educated women tend to have their first child at a later age than less educated women. Secondly, women who proceed later to have another child have had their first child earlier in life than women who are observed only to have had a first birth. This pattern is true within each educational group and across educational groups for all three countries, except for more highly educated Swedish women. Also the women who were observed to have three children in the data had their first child at a still younger age than those who were observed to have two children.

Comparing our three countries we observe some consistent differences. Women in Great Britain become mothers at a younger age than either in Germany or in Sweden. In Great Britain because benefits are small less educated women have less reason to think about obtaining a right to a maternity benefit than is the case in Germany and Sweden. This may lead to earlier motherhood among less educated British women in comparison to German and Swedish women. However as in the other two countries, more highly educated women in Britain have to consider their labour market prospects and this induces postponement of motherhood as explained in section 6.2. The relatively brief job guarantee period in Britain might make having a child more costly in career terms than would be the case if the job protection period was larger because a mother may have to give up her job and find a new one before she can return to paid employment. Consequently British women are forced to pay more attention to the career costs of having children. Demographic trends in all three countries have shown a rise in the age of first-time mothers over time. Since the British data period starts earlier and therefore covers 1980-1992 different from Sweden and Germany for which the data start in 1984, British mothers on average are expected to be slightly younger out of the demographic reason.

One of our theoretical predictions implies that other things equal, the higher husband's income, the earlier the birth of the first child. The theoretical variable for the influence of husband's income is the present value of his life-time earnings which is not available. Therefore we use predicted income at age 40 following Willis (1973) for the Swedish and the German data for which we have information on husband's income at the birth of the first child and his age at this point in time. However the effect of husband's income at age 40 on the timing of motherhood is positive and statistically significant for Sweden which means that the higher husband's income, the later first birth – contrary to economic theory. The variable husband's schooling is meant to capture his education and career planning and we find that there is an effect independent of income, for Germany and Great Britain, but not for Sweden. In Britain first births are timed later the higher the husband's level of education and the higher his positioning on a seven-steps occupational ladder (used because husband's income is not available for 1980-1990). For all three countries we found when husband's income and education are held constant, the more well-educated the woman the longer she postpones motherhood.

Clustering births or second career break?

The time it takes before entering into paid work after giving birth is not influenced by whether the woman enters into part-time or full-time employment. This is true for both Germany and Sweden. In both countries a large majority of mothers choose part-time employment rather than full-time employment. This is true for 63% across categories in Germany and for 75% in Sweden. For Great Britain the data do not allow to make this distinction. Swedish mothers are assisted in this choice by family policies because parents have a legal right to shorten work hours to six hours a day until their child is eight years old, and then return to full-time in the same job.

One interesting similarity across countries is that women who enter the labour market between births do so after about 12 months in all three countries, although the job protection period varies between countries. This might lead one to posit a biologically and emotionally optimum of 12 months full-time baby care coupled with a subsequent return to work on a - part-time basis. One difference between Sweden and the other two countries is that a greater proportion of Swedish first time mothers re-enter the labour market between first and second births: 35% in Germany and 39% in Great Britain compared to 47% in Sweden. Although Swedish parents have a right to the extend to another 18 months parental leave when the second child is born within 30 months of the third, this does not mean that they could not enter the labour market during 36 months (18 months for the first child and 18 months for the second child) of leave. Swedish parents are allowed to interrupt leave in order to save days for later use.

Sweden also differs from the other two countries in that the duration of time out of the labour market is about one year both for the women for whom we observe only the first birth and for women who re-enter between births. For women who do not re-enter the labour market between the first and the second birth the duration of home time is about three and a half to five years.

In Germany and Great Britain the younger the mother is at the birth of the first child the less eager she is to enter paid employment afterwards. In Germany and Great Britain, women with more human capital accumulated at time of first birth spend less time at home since both education of the mother and years of experience of the mother have a positive effect on the number of months before entering paid employment. This effect is in line with our expectations that women with more human capital should be more eager to return to paid work.

Theoretical considerations on optimal age at maternity

In Chapter 7 we are interested in the planning problem of young women: when is the right time to give birth considering their life time earnings? We intend to measure the direct costs and the human capital investments loss for different patterns of hours and participation during different lengths of labour market spells of women after having had their first child. In the simulations we fully concentrate on women and assume that husband's income has not an influence. Since women have different market productivity because of different educational attainment and different number of years of experience, the career costs differ by women's age at having their first child (as laid out in chapter 6).

Career costs consist on the one hand of direct loss of earnings due to leaving the labour market to give birth and care for a new born child and on the other hand the loss of returns until retirement because of human capital investments not undertaken during a period of home time.

Which is the relevant potential earnings curve in the planning problem of a future mother? We believe that current and prospective caring tasks are the main explanatory factor in the male/female wage gap. The relevant potential earnings against which the woman will judge her career prospects is the age earnings curve on average of narrowly defined educational groups. Therefore men's age earnings curves will be used as potential earnings for a woman in her planning decision for the timing of maternity. We showed that women's prebirth wages are rather similar to those of men.

A second assumption which is empirically confirmed is that the wage that a woman receives by return to work after a period of home time is the same as that which she earned before leaving her job for childbearing and infant care.

Simulations of life time earnings loss in The Netherlands of having the first child at different ages

We simulate the life time earnings loss by varying assumptions on years of home time, probability of labour force participation in the post maternity period and varying hours of work in the post maternity period. The number of years of home time in connection with childbirth are assumed to be either 1, 4 or 10 years. In some simulations we use information on probability of labour force participation one wave (two years) after first birth for women who gave birth to their first child in the period 1990-1996 by educational group and information on hours of work for women who were employed one survey after giving birth to their first child. The labour force participation of the 1990 generation of Dutch mothers is much larger than those of the 1980 generation of Dutch mothers and we believe that future mothers who now have to make this planning decision are more likely to behave like the 1990 generation. Life time earnings loss is expressed as a fraction of potential life time earnings discounted back to age 23. We do the simulations for three educational groups high, medium and low educated.

    If you plan to be a full time home maker during 10 years the life time earnings loss will be about 24% of potential life time earnings if you have your child at age 35 in comparison to having a child at 23 which means a loss of 31% of potential life time earnings. If part time work becomes a life long behaviour in the post maternity period the earnings loss will be 30 to 50% of potential earnings for all educational groups. There are big differences in observed employment probabilities and the life time earnings loss by applying observed values will therefore vary between educational groups. Whereas high educated women lose at a maximum 40.5% of potential life time earnings the loss always amounts to more than 45% for low educated women with a maximum of 77.1% for a low educated woman who decides to have a child at age 23 stay out for 10 years full time and then have the observed probability of becoming employed afterwards.

    If the probability of employment and hours of work of employed women will remain the same for the whole post maternity period until retirement the life time earnings loss will vary across educational groups with low educated women losing at least 56% of potential life time earnings and at most 88.5% and high educated women losing a minimum of 33.7% and a maximum of 65.1%. Losses of this magnitude have been the rule for Dutch women of earlier cohorts (Dankmeijer, 1996, Mertens, 1998).

In all the simulations where part time work continues for the whole post maternity period the loss of potential life time earnings is substantial and the loss is always smaller the later the woman enters into maternity.

Life time earnings gain by postponement of first birth

For all three educational groups comparing the 1980s to the 1990s postponement of first birth in The Netherlands has been substantial. Also more educated women have their children later than less educated women. Women with medium or low education have postponed their first child's birth beyond age 27 to a very large extent comparing the 1980s to the 1990s. Whereas 70% of these women had their first child by age 27 in the 1980s the percentage had decreased to 45% for women with medium education and to 54% for women with low education. The distribution of first births to high educated women is pushed further into older first time mothers. In the 1980s by age 31 as many as 83% had become mothers but in the 1990s this same proportion was reached not before age 33. As many as 14% of the first time mothers with high education had their first birth after age 35 in the 1990s. The postponement of motherhood across educational groups is presented in the last two columns of Table 7.3. Whereas in the 1980s by age 31 there remained 9% of first births yet to come this was the case for 19% of first births in the 1990s.

Women have been rational in delaying first birth. If the pattern of mother's age at first child birth of the 1980s had prevailed into the 1990s 17% more women would have given birth by age 23. Now instead they postpone first birth say to age 27 and therefore lose 44.3% of potential life time earnings instead of 50.2%. Another 23% according to Table 7.3 would have given birth by age 27 if the age pattern of birth giving had remained the same in the 1990s as it was in the 1980s. This means that their life time earnings loss is reduced to 38.6% from 44.3% of potential life time earnings. There are therefore substantial gains to be made by postponement of birth.

If however it may be the case that the 1990 generation of Dutch women will reenter full time employment after an extended period of half time work the earnings loss will be limited. Say that our medium educated woman works 21 hours per week during four years and then returns to full time work. Her life time earnings loss will then be limited to 4.4. to 6.4% of potential life time earnings and the maximum gain of postponement is only 2% of potential life time earnings. For such a woman there is consequently no big issue to have a child by age 27 rather than wait until age 35, when chances of becoming pregnant decrease and other complications may arise.

Medical costs associated with postponement of births would in principle offset the costs of life time earnings loss as would also the costs of day care which the mother otherwise would do as unpaid work at home. Costs of using biomedical techniques for conception is one aspect of such costs. Other aspects of costs are associated with health of children and health of mothers. It is known that the risk of being born with Down syndrome increases as the mother is older. We do not know if older mothers are observed to have more health risks in connection with births but if this is the case such costs should also be included.

In the setting of the Dutch 1990s subsidised day care is available to a limited extent, but Statistics Netherlands (1993) shows that on average parents still pay 28%. In addition market priced day care for children is expensive to families. Given individual taxes, day care fees and the legal right to keep a job on a part time basis it is an economically attractive option for the couple to share: mother cares for the child at home one day and works 4 days, father cares for the child at home a different day, childcare is paid for 3 days or maybe even 2 days if there is a grandmother who volunteers for one day a week, a situation that would not be unusual given the fact that within the generation of women with adult children more than 50% are housewives (OSA,Kunnen et al. 1997). Results of Rönsen and Sundström (1996) comparing family policies of Sweden and Norway over time show that the longer the job protection period the sooner recent mothers return to work because more mothers can arrange satisfactory day care for a one year old or 18 months year old child than for a two months old child. This implies that a longer job protection period would probably result in more Dutch mothers keeping their jobs after maternity, which is a factor that decreases life time earnings loss and therefore decreases the gains of postponement of maternity. Whereas there is an economic rational for working part time during periods when day care costs are paid the economics of continuing to work part time when such costs are not any more paid are different. However if as the goal is for Dutch equal opportunity policies a shorter work week will apply in equal amount for men and women this is a life quality gain for the society.

Bibliography

Albrecht J.W., P.A. Edin, M. Sundström and S.B. Vroman (1997), *Career Interruptions and Subsequent Earnings: A Reexamination Using Swedish Data*, Paper Presented To The European Society of Population Economics.

Allaart P.C., R. Kunnen, J.C. Van Ours and H.A. Van Stiphout (1987), *OSA Trendrapport 1987, Actuele Informatie Over De Arbeidsmarkt*, OSA Voorstudie Nr V 18, The Hague.

Allaart P.C., R. Kunnen, W.C.M. Praat, H.A. Van Stiphout, and J.P.M. Vosse (1991), *OSA Trendrapport Aanbod Van Arbeid 1991*, OSA Rapport Nr 12, The Hague.

Arachne (1994), Invloed; Informatie voor/over Vrouwen en Overheidsbeleid 2,11.

Arbeidsinspectie (1997), *Emancipatie in Cao's*, Ministerie van Sociale Zaken en Werkgelegenheid, April.

Aronsson T. and J. Walker (1995), *The Effects of Sweden's Welfare State On Labour Supply Incentives*, Sns Occasional Chapter No. 64, January, Stockholm.

Bakker B.F.M., K.G. Tijdens and J.W. Winkels (1997), *Integrating Occupational Segregation and Human Capital in the Explanation of the (Dutch) Gender Wage Gap*, Manuscript, University of Amsterdam.

Becker G.S. (1981), *A Treatise On The Family*, Cambridge, Mass.: Harvard University Press.

Becker G.S., E.M. Landes and R.T. Michael (1977), An Economic Analysis of Marital Instability, *Journal of Political Economy* 88.

Beets G., A. Bouwens and J. Schippers (1997), *Uitgesteld Ouderschap*, Thesis Publishers, Amsterdam.

Bekkering J.M., Y.K. Grift and J.J. Siegers (1986), *Belasting en Premieheffing en de Arbeidsmarktparticipatie door Gehuwde Vrouwen. Een Econometrische Analyse*, Ministerie Van Sociale Zaken en Werkgelegenheid, The Hague.

Berkel Van M. and N.D. De Graaf (1995), Economische Afhankelijkheid Van Gehuwde Vrouwen in Nederland, 1979-1991, *Mens en Maatschappy* 70 (2), Mei: 138-151.

Bettio F. and P. Villa (1996), *A Mediterranean Perspective On The Break-Down of The Relationship Between Participation and Fertility*, Universita Degli Studi Di Trento Dipartimento Di Economica, Discussion Paper No.5.

Blau F. and A. Grossberg (1990), *Maternal Labour Supply and Children's Cognitive Development*, Nber Working Paper No 3535. Cambridge, Mass.: National Bureau of Economic Research.

171

Blossfeld H.P. and J. Huinink (1991), Human Capital Investments Or Norms of Role Transition? How Women's Schooling and Career Affect the Process of Family Formation, *American Journal of Sociology* 97: 143-168.

Blundell R. (1993), *Taxation and Labour Supply: Incentives in the UK*, In: Atkinson A. and V. Mogensen (Eds), *Welfare and Work Incentives*, Oxford: Clarendon Press.

Bonsel G.J. and P.J. Van Der Maas (Red.) (1994), *Aan De Wieg Van De Toekomst; Scenario's Voor De Zorg Rond De Menselijke Voortplanting, 1995-2010.* Houten: Stafleu Van Loghum.

Bouwens A. (1996), *Uitgesteld Ouderschap*, Emancipatieraad, The Hague.

Brown J. and S. Small (1991), *Maternity Benefits*. London: The Public Policy Institute.

Carlin P.S. and L. Flood (1997), Do Children Affect the Labour Supply of Swedish Men: Time Diary Vs. Survey Data, *Labour Economics* 4: 167-83.

CBS (1985,1998), *Statistical Yearbook*, Voorburg/Heerlen.

CBS (1991), *Kindercentra 1991*. The Hague: Staatsuitgeverij, Centraal Bureau Voor De Statistiek.

CBS (1994), *Relatie en Gezinsvorming in De Jaren Negentig*, Voorburg/Heerlen.

CBS (1996), *Employment and Wages in 1994*, Voorburg/Heerlen.

CBS/CPB, *Population and Labour Supply: Three Scenario's Till 2020*, The Hague: Sdu, 1997.

CDA (1997), *De Verzwegen Keuze Van Nederland. Naar Een Christen-Democratisch Familie en Gezinsbeleid*. Wetenschappelijk Bureau Voor Het CDA, The Hague.

Chiswick C.U. and E.L. Lehrer (1990), On Marriage Specific Human Capital. Its Role As Determinant of Remarriage, *Journal of Population Economics* 3, 193-213.

Cigno A. (1991), *Economics of the Family*, Oxford: Clarendon Press.

Cigno A. and J.F. Ermisch (1989), A Microeconomic Analysis of the Timing of Births *European Economic Review* 33, North Holland: 737-760.

Cohen B. and K. Clarke (1986), *Child Care and Equal Opportunities*, London: HMSO.

Cohen B. (1988), *Caring For Children: Services and Policies For Child Care and Equal Opportunities in the UK*. Report For the European Commisssion's Child Care Network, London: Family Policies Centre.

Cohen B. (1990), *Caring For Children. the 1990 Report*. Report For the European Commission's Child Care Network, London: Family Policies Centre.

Corcoran M. and G. Duncan (1979), Work History, Labour Force Attachment and Earnings Differences Between the Races and Sexes, *Journal of Human Resources* 14 (1), Winter.

Corti L., H. Laurie and S. Dex. (1994), *Caring and Employment*, Employment Department Research Series No 39.

Council of Europe (1993), *Recent Demographic Developments in Europe and North America 1992*, Council of Europe Press Strasbourg.

Council of Europe (1996), *Recent Demographic Developments in Europe and North America*, Council of Europe Press Strassbourg.

Cuyvers P., K. De Hoog and H. Pott-Buter (1997), *Gezinsbeleid in Perspectief*, In: Grotenhuis S. and J. Van Der Zwaard (Eds), *Kiezen Voor Kinderen*, Utrecht: Elsevier/ De Tijdstroom/ Nederlandse Gezinsraad.

Dale A. and H. Joshi (1992), *The Economic and Social Status of British Women*. In: Butler, G., G. Heilig and G. Schmidtt-Rink (Eds.), *Acta Demographica*, Heidelberg: Physica Verlag: 27-46.

Daniel W.W. (1980), *Maternity Rights: The Experience of Women*. London: Policy Studies Institute.

Dankmeijer B. (1996), Long Run Opportunity Costs of Children According To Education of the Mother in The Netherlands, *Journal of Population Economics* 9 No 3: 349-361.

De Beer J. (1997), *Vruchtbaarheid: Trends en Prognose*. Maandstatistiek Van De Bevolking CBS 1997/7: 15-25.

De Jong A.H (1994), *Ontwikkeling in the Arbeidsparticipatie Van Moeders*, Maandstatistiek Van De Bevolking CBS November 1994: 6-18.

Deutscher Bundestag (1990), Unterrichtung Durch Die Bundesregierung: *Bericht Über Die in Den Jahren 1986 Bis 1988 Gemachten Erfahrungen Mit Dem Gesetz Über Die Gewährung Von Erziehungsgeld Und Erziehungsurlaub*. Bundesdrucksache 11/8517, Bonn.

Deutscher Bundestag (1991), *Ubersicht Über Die Soziale Sicherheit*. Bundesdrucksache, Bonn.

Deutscher Bundestag (1991), Unterrichtung Durch Die Bundesregierung: *Bericht Der Bundesregierung Zur Frage Weitere Maßnahmen Der Frauenförderung in Beruf, Familie Und anderen Bereichen*. Bundesdrucksache 12/447, Bonn.

Dex S. (1984), *Women's Work Histories: An Analysis of the Women and Employment Survey*, Research Paper No. 46, London: Department of Employment.

Dex S. (1987), *Women's Occupational Mobility*, London: Macmillan.

Dex S. (1991), *The Reliability of Recall Data: A Literature Review*, Working Paper 11 of the Esrc, Research Centre On Micro-Social Change in Britain, Colchester: University of Essex.

Dex S., P. Walters and M. Arden (1993), *French and British Mothers At Work*, London: Macmillan.

Ditch J., H. Barnes, J. Bradshaw, J. Comaille and T. Eardley (1994), *A Synthesis of National Family Policies 1994*, European Observatory On National Family Policies.

Ditch J., J. Bradshaw and T. Eardley (1994), *Developments in National Family Policies 1994, European Observatory On National Family Policies*, European Observatory On National Family Policies.

Dobbelsteen S.H.A.M., Gustafsson S.S., C.M.M.P. Wetzels, Childcare in The Netherlands between government, firms and parents. Is the dead weight loss smaller than in the public daycare system of Sweden, working paper.

EOC (Equal Opportunities Commission) (1991), *Women and Men in Britain 1991*, London: HMSO.

Esping-Andersen G. (1990), *The Three Worlds of Welfare Capitalism*. Princeton: Princeton University Press.

Esping-andersen G. (1996), After The Golden Age? Welfare State Dilemmas in A Global Economy, In G. Esping andersen (Ed.), *Welfare States in Transition, National Adaptations in Global Economies*, United Nations Research Institute For Social Development, Sage Publications: 1-31.

Fauser (1998), Inaugurale Rede als Hoogleraar Gynaecologische Endocrinologie, Erasmus Universiteit, Rotterdam, 29 Januari.

Flood L., A. Klevmarken and P.Olovsson (1993), *Hushållens Ekonomiska Levnadsförhållenden, 1993 Årsundersöckning*, Nationalekonomiska, Uppsala: Uppsala Universitet.

Freedman D. et al (1988), The Life History Calendar: A Technique For Collecting Retrospective Data, *Sociological Methodology*: 37-68.

Gregg P. and J. Wadsworth (1995), *More Work In Fewer Households?*, Discussion Paper 72, National Institute of Economic and Social Research.

Groot W. and H. Pott-Buter (1992), The Timing of Maternity in The Netherlands, *Journal of Population Economics* 5: 155-172.

Groot W. and J. Van Ours (1994), *Career Interruptions and Subsequent Earnings.* Tinbergen Discussion Chapter TI 94-6, Amsterdam/Rotterdam: Tinbergen Institute.

Groot W. and H. Maassen Van Den Brink (1996), *Monitoring Kinderopvang, Veranderingen in Het Gebruik Van Kinderopvang, 1991-1995.* Rijswijk: Ministerie Van Volksgezondheid, Welzijn en Sport.

Groot W. and H. Maassen Van Den Brink (1997), *Verlate Uittreding, Oorzaken Van Uittreding Uit Het Arbeidsproces Ruim Na De Geboorte Van Het Eerste Kind.* Onderzoek in Opdracht Van Het Ministerie Van Sociale Zaken en Werkgelegenheid, Augustus, VUGA, The Hague.

Groves, D. (1983), *Members and Survivors: Women and Retirement Legislation*, In: Lewis J. (Ed.), *Women's Welfare, Women's Rights.* London: Croom Helm.

Gustafsson B. and A.N Klevmarken (1993), *Taxes and Transfers in Sweden: Incentive Effects On Labour Supply* In: Atkinson A. and V. Mogensen (Eds), *Welfare and Work Incentives*, Clarendon Press, Oxford.

Gustafsson B. and U. Kjullin (1994), Time Use in Child Care and Housework and the Total Costs of Children, *Journal of Population Economics* 7 (3): 287-306.

Gustafsson S.S. (1981), *Male-Female Lifetime Earnings Differentials and Labour Force History*, In: Eliasson, Holmlund, Stafford, F. (Eds.) *Studies in Labour Market Behavior, Sweden and the United States*, the Industrial Institute For Economic and Social Research, Conference Reports, Stockholm.

Gustafsson S.S. (1984), *Equal Opportunity Policies in Sweden*, In: G.Schmid and R. Weitzel (Eds.), *Sex Discrimination and Equal Opportunity. the Labour Market and Employment Policy*. Wissenschaftzentrum, London: West Berlin and Gower Publishing Company.

Gustafsson S.S. (1992), Cohort Size and Female Labour Supply, *European Journal of Population* 8: 1-21.

Gustafsson S.S. (1992), 'Separate Taxation and Married Women's Labour Supply, A Comparison of West Germany and Sweden, *Journal of Population Economics* 5: 61-85.

Gustafsson S.S. (1994), *Child Care and Types of Welfare States* In: Sainsbury, D. (Ed.), *Gendering Welfare States*, London: Sage Publications.

Gustafsson S.S. and M. Bruyn-Hundt (1991), Incentives for Women to Work: A Comparison between The Netherlands, Sweden and West Germany, *Journal of Economic Studies* 18 (5/6): 30-66.

Gustafsson S.S. and F. Stafford (1992), Child Care Subsidies and Labour Supply in Sweden, *Journal of Human Resources* 27 (1): 204-230.

Gustafsson S.S. and F. Stafford (1994), *Three Regimes of Child Care*, In: R. Blank (Ed.), *Social Protection Versus Economic Flexibility: Is There A Tradeoff?* Chicago: National Bureau of Economic Research and University of Chicago Press: 333-361.

Gustafsson S.S. and F. Stafford (1995), *Equity and Efficiency Trade-offs in Early Childhood Care and Education*, Mimeo, University of Amsterdam.

Gustafsson S.S., C.M.M.P. Wetzels, J.D. Vlasblom and S. Dex (1996), Labour Force Transitions in Connection With Child Birth A Panel Data Comparison Between Germany, Great Britain and Sweden, *Journal of Population Economics* 9: 223-246.

Gustafsson S.S. and C.M.M.P. Wetzels (1997), *Paid Careers and the Timing and Spacing of Births in Germany, Great Britain and Sweden.* In: Tijdens K.G., Doorne-Huiskes A. Van and Willemsen T. *Time Allocation and Gender. The Relationship Between Paid Labour and Household Work*. Tilburg University Press 99-122.

Gustafsson S.S. and C.M.M.P. Wetzels (2000), *Optimal Age At Giving First Birth: Germany, Great Britain, The Netherlands and Sweden.* in Gustafsson S.S. and Meulders D.E.. *Gender and the Labour Market. Econometric Evidence on Obstacles in Achieving Gender Equality*. Macmillan, London, p.188-209.

Gustafsson S.S., C.M.M.P. Wetzels and E. Kenjoh (Forthcoming), Can Postponement of Maternity in the 1990s Be Explained out of Time Spent out of Market Work, Panel Data Analyses Comparing the 1990s to the 1980s Across Germany, Great Britain, The Netherlands and Sweden, *Journal of Public Finance and Management.*

Gustafsson S.S., E. Kenjoh and C.M.M.P. Wetzels (Forthcoming), The Role of Education in Postponement of Maternity in Britain, Germany, The Netherlands

176   *Squeezing Birth into Working Life*

and Sweden, in Dale A. and E. Ruspini (eds), Engendering Longitudinal Analysis, The Policy Press.

Heckman J.J., V.J. Hotz and J.R. Walker (1985), New Evidence On the Timing and Spacing of Births, *AEA Papers and Proceeding* 75 (2): 179-184.

Heckman J.J. and J.R. Walker (1990), The Relationship Between Wages and Income and the Timing and Spacing of Births: Evidence From Swedish Longitudinal Data, *Econometrica* 58, (6): 1411-1441.

Hoem B. (1996), *Some Features of Recent Demographic Trends in Sweden*, Stockholm Research Reports in Demography, No 104, April.

Hoem J.M. (1993), Public Policy As the Fuel of Fertility: Effects of A Policy Reform On the Pace of Childbearing in Sweden in the 1980s, *Acta Sociologica* 36: 19-31.

Hupe P.L. (1993), Beyond Pillarization: The (Post) Welfare State in The Netherlands, *European Journal of Political Research*, 23(4) Annual Review: 359-386.

Jenkins S.P. (1994), *Winners and Losers: A Portrait of the UK Income Distribution During the 1980's*. Discussion Paper 94-107, Department of Economics, University College Wales, Swansea.

Joshi H. (1990), The Cash Alternative Costs of Childbearing: An Approach To Estimation Using British Data, *Population Studies* 44:41-60.

Joshi H. and P.R.A. Hinde (1993), Employment After Childbearing in Post-War Britain: Cohort Study Evidence On Contrasts Within and Across Generations, *European Sociological Review* 9: 203-227.

Joshi H., S. Macran and S. Dex (1996), Employment After Childbearing and Women's Subsequent Labour Force Participation: Evidence From the British 1958 Birth Cohort, *Journal of Population Economics* 9: 325-348.

Killingsworth M. and J.J. Heckman (1986), *Female Labour Supply*, In: Ashenfelter, O. and R. Layard Eds, *Handbook of Labour Economics*, North Holland, Amsterdam: 103-204.

Klevmarken A. and P. Olovsson (1993), *Household Market and Nonmarket Activities: Procedures and Codes 1994-1991*, Stockholm: Almqvist & Wiksell International.

Kunnen R., W.C.M. Praat, A.M. De Voogd-Hamelink, C.M.M.P. Wetzels (1997), *Trendrapport Aanbod Van Arbeid 1997*, OSA-Rapport Nr.25, Mei.

Land H. (1985), *Who Still Cares For the Family? Recent Developments in Income Maintenance, Taxation and Family Law*, In: C. Ungerson (Ed.), *Women and Social Policy: A Reader*. London: Macmillan.

Leerentveld (1993), Tien Jaar Ivf in Nederland. *Medisch Contact* 48: 1531-1536.

Leibowitz A., J.A. Klerman and L.J. Waite (1992), Employment of New Mothers and Child Care Choice, *Journal of Human Resources* 27: 112-133.

Luijn Van H. (1996), *Het Vrouwelijk Dilemma*, Leiden: Dswo Press.

Luijn Van H. and A. Parent (1990), *Laatste Kans Moeders*, Delft: Eburon 1990, Nisso Studie 8.

Maassen Van Den Brink H. and W. Groot (1995), *Kinderopvang en Arbeidsparticipatie in Nederland*, In: H. Maassen Van Den Brink, S.S. Gustafsson and W. Groot, *Kinderopvang tussen Markt en Overheid*, Amsterdam: Welboom: 33-48.

Malthus, T.R [1798] (1976). *An Essay On the Principle of Population*, By A. Flew(Ed.).

Martin J. and C. Roberts (1984), *Women and Employment: A Life-Time Perspective*, Department of Employment/OPCS, London: HMSO.

Mcrae S. (1991), *Maternity Rights in Britain*, London: Policy Studies Institute.

Mcrae S. (1996), *Women's Employment During Family Formation*, London: Policy Studies Institute.

Mertens E.H.M. (1998), Loopbaanonderbrekingen en Kinderen: Gevolgen Voor De Beloning Van Vrouwen, Doctoral Dissertation, University of Utrecht.

Mincer J. (1962), *Labour Force Participation of Married Women* In: H. Gregg Lewis (Ed.), *Aspects of Labour Economics*, Universities National Bureau Conference Series 14. Princeton, N. J.: Princeton University Press.

Mincer, J. (1963), *Market Prices, Opportunity Costs, and Income Effects*, In: C. Christ, M. Friedman, L. Goodman, Z. Griliches, A. Harbenger, N. Leviatan, J.Mincer, Y. Mundlak, M. Nerlove, D. Patinkin, L. Telser and H. Theil (Eds.), *Measurement in Economics: Studies in Mathematical Economics and Econometrics in Memory of Yehuda Grunfeld*, Stanford, California: Stanford University Press.

Mincer J. (1974), *Schooling, Experience and Earnings*, New York and London: Columbia University Press.

Mincer J. and H. Ofek (1982), Interrupted Work Careers, *Journal of Human Resources* 17:3-24.

Mincer J. and S. Polacheck (1974), Family Investments in Human Capital: Earnings of Women, *Journal of Political Economy*, 82(2): 76-108.

Ministry of Social Affairs and Employment (1997), *Kansen op Combineren, Arbeid, Zorg en Economische Zelfstandigheid*, September.

Moree M. (1992), *Mijn kinderen hebben er niets van gemerkt, Buitenshuis Werkende Vrouwen Tussen 1950 en Nu*. Utrecht: Jan Van Arkel.

Moss P. (1988). *Child Care and Equality of Opportunity*, Consolidated Report To the European Commission, Eec Report V/746/88-En.

Moss P. (1990). *Child Care in the European Community 1985-1990*, Women in Europe, Supplements No 31.

Mutsaers H.P.M. (1997), *Kinderopvang in Gemeenten in De Periode 1989-1995*, The Hague: Vereniging Van Nederlandse Gemeenten.

Myrdal A. and G. Myrdal (1934), *Kris I Befolkningsfrågan*, Stockholm.

National Insurance Board (1989), *Föräldralpenning Med Anledning Av Barns Födelse Avseende 1988. Statistik Information Is-I 1989*: 24, National Insurance Board, Stockholm.

178   *Squeezing Birth into Working Life*

National Insurance Board (1990), *Uttag Av Föraldrapenning Med Anledning Av Barns Födelse Under Barnets Första Levnadår. Statistik Information Isi 1990*: 16 National Insurance Board, Stockholm.

Nelson J.A. (1991), Tax Reform and Feminist Theory in the United States: Incorporating Human Connection, *Journal of Economic Studies*, Volume 18: 5/6: 11-30.

Nerlove M. and A. Razin (1981), In: A. Deaton (Ed.) *Essays On the Theory and Measurement of Consumer Behaviour*, in Honour of Sir R.Stone, Cambridge: Cambridge University Press.

Ni Bhrolchain M. (1983), *Birth Spacing and Women's Work: Some British Evidence*, Lshtm Centre For Population Studies Research Paper No. 83-3.

Ni Bhrolchain M. (1985a), Birth Intervals and Women's Economic Activity: Some British Evidence, *Journal of Biosocial Science* 17: 31-4.

Ni Bhrolchain M. (1986a), Women's Paid Work and the Timing of Births: Longitudinal Evidence, *European Journal of Population* 2: 43-70.

Niphuis Nell M. (1997), In: Beets, G., A. Bouwens, J. Schippers (Eds.), *Uitgesteld Ouderschap*, Amsterdan: Thesis Publishers.

Oaxaca R.L. (1973), Male-Female Wage Differentials in Urban Labour Markets, *International Economic Review* 9: 693-709.

OECD [Organisation For Economic Cooperation and Development] (1995), *Economic Outlook 58*, December. Paris: OECD.

OECD (1990), *Employment Outlook*. Paris: OECD.

Ondrich J., K. Spiess and Q. Yang (1996), Barefoot and in A German Kitchen: Federal Parental Leave and Benefit Policy and the Return To Work After Childbirth in Germany, *Journal of Population Economics* 9: 247-266.

Ophem H. Van and N. Jonker (1996), *The Duration of Higher Education*, Tinbergen Institute Discussion Paper, Ti 96-158/3.

OSA [Organisatie Voor Strategisch Arbeidsmarkt Onderzoek] [Institute For Labour Studies] (1991,1997), See Allaart et al, Kunnen et al.

Ostner I. (1993), *Slow Motion: Women, Work and the Family in Germany*, In: Lewis, Jane (Ed.) *Women and Social Policy in Europe*, Aldershot England: Edward Elgar Publishing Ltd.

Praat W.C.M. and E. Mekkelholt (1991), Intern Document OSA.

Queen's Speech 1998, *Hoofdpunten Van Het Regeringsbeleid 1999* (1998), The Hague: SDU Uitgevers.

ROA [Researchcentrum Voor Onderwijs en Arbeidsmarkt] [Research Center For Education and the Labour Market] 1997, De Arbeidsmarkt Naar Opleiding en Beroepsgroep 7.

Rönsen M. and M. Sundström (1995), Maternal Employment in Nordic Countries. A Comparison of the After-Birth Employment Activity of Norwegian and Swedish Women, *Journal of Population Economics* 9: 267-285.

Rönsen M. and M. Sundström (1996), Women's Return To Work After First Birth in the Nordic Countries--Full-Time Or Part-Time?, Paper Presented at ESPE, June 13-15.

Sainsbury D. (1994), *Gendering Welfare States*, London: Sage Publications.

Sainsbury D. (1996), *Gender, Equality and Welfare States*, Cambridge University Press.

Schultz T.P. (1973), A Preliminary Survey of Economic Analyses of Fertility, *American Economic Review* 63: 71-87.

Schultz T.P. (1981), *Economics of Population*, Preindustrial Equilibrium: A Mathusian Perspective, Addison Wesley Publishing Company: 9-31.

SCP [Social and Cultural Planning office] (1997), Gezinsrapport. Rijswijk: The Netherlands.

SCP (1997) Sociale Atlas Van De Vrouw, Deel 4, Rijswijk, The Netherlands.

Socialstyrelsen (1995), Barnomsorgen 1994 (Childcare 1994), Stockholm.

Sörensen A. and A. Mclanahan (1987), Married Women's Economic Dependency 1940-1980, *American Journal of Sociology* 93 (3): 659-87.

Spaans J. (1997), *Tussen Wens en Realiteit. Onderzoek naar de Wijze waarop Mannelijke Werknemers hun Deeltijdwens en/of Wens tot Calamiteitenverlof Realiseren en de Belemmeringen daarbij*, Ministerie Van Sociale Zaken en Werkgelegenheid. The Hague: Vuga.

Statistics Netherlands, See CBS.

Statistics Sweden (1989), SCB Befolkningsstatistik, Barnomsorgundersökningen 1989, S11sm 8901, Stockholm.

Statistics Sweden (1992), SCB Befolkningsstatistik Del 4, Stockholm.

Statistics Sweden (1998), Labour Force Statistics.

Statistisches Bundesambt (Various Issues), Fachserie 1: Bevölkerung Und Erwerbstätigkeit.

Sundström M. (1996), Determinants of the Use of Parental Leave Benefits By Women in Sweden in the 1990s, *Scandinavian Journal of Social Welfare* 5: 76-82.

Sundström M. and F. Stafford (1992), Female Labour Force Participation, Fertility and Public Policy in Sweden, *European Journal of Population* 8: 199-215.

Tasiran A.C. (1993), *Wage and Income Effects On the Timing and Spacing of Births in Sweden and the United States*, Doctoral Dissertation, University of Gotenborg.

Taylor M. (Ed.) (1992), *British Household Panel Survey User Manual*, Volumes A and B, Essex University Esrc Research Centre On Micro-Social Change.

Therborn G. (1989), *Pillarization and Popular Movements: Two Variants of Welfare State Capitalism: The Netherlands and Sweden*, In: F.G. Castles (Eds), *The Comparative History of Public Policy*. Cambridge: Polity Press.

Tijdens, K.G. and S. Lioen (1993), *Kinderopvang in Nederland, Organisatie en Financiering*, Utrecht: Jan Van Arkel.

Vermeulen H., S. Dex, T. Callan, B. Dankmeyer, S. Gustafsson, M. Lausten, N. Smith, G. Schmauss and J.D. Vlasblom (1994), *Tax Systems and Married Women's Labour Force Participation: A Seven Country Comparison*, Working Paper of the EC Human Capital and Mobility Female Labour Force Network.

Vlasblom J.D. (1998), *Differences in Labour Supply and Income of Women in The Netherlands and the Federal Republic of Germany: A Comparative Analysis of the Effect of Taxes and Social Premiums*, Doctoral Dissertation, University of Utrecht.

Wagner G.G., J. Schupp and U. Rendtel (1991), *The Socio-Economic Panel of Germany, Methods of Production and Management of Longitudinal Data*, Diw Discussion Paper 31a, Berlin.

Wagner G.G., R. Burckhauser and F. Behringer (1993), The English Language Public Use File of the German Socio-Economic Panel, *Journal of Human Resources* 28 (2):429-433.

Ward C., A. Dale and H. Joshi (1996), Combining Employment With Childcare: An Escape From Dependence? *Journal of Social Policy* 25: 223-247.

Wetzels C.M.M.P. (1994), *Geloof, Passie, Graan en Kindervreugd, De Relatie Van Malthus' Bevolkingstheorie met de Economische Theorie van de Vruchtbaarheid*, In: H. Maassen Van Den Brink and K.G. Tijdens (Eds.) *Emancipatie en Economie: Is Nederland Een Land Waar Vrouwen Willen Wonen?*, Amsterdam: Spinhuis: 127-157.

Wilensky H. (1982), *Leftism, Catholicism and Democratic Corporatism: The Role of Parties in Recent Welfare State Development*, In: P. Flora and H. Heidenheimer (Eds), *The Developments of Welfare States in Europe and North America*. New Brunswick, Nj: Transaction Books.

Willis R.J. (1973), A New Approach to the Economic Theory of Fertility Behaviour, *Journal of Political Economy* 81 (2) Part Ii:S14-S64.

Willis R.J. (1974), *Economic Theory of Fertility Behavior*, In: *Economics of the Family*. Edited By T.W. Schultz. Chicago: University of Chicago Press.

Zimmermann K.F. (1993), *Responses to Taxes and Benefits in Germany*, In: Atkinson A.B. and Mogensen G.V. (Eds.), *Welfare and Work Incentives. A North European Perspective*, Oxford: Clarendon Press: 192-240.